SAN QUENTIN

THE EVOLUTION OF A CALIFORNIA STATE PRISON

Edited by

Bonnie L. Petry

and

Michael Burgess

A Sidewinder Book

Borgo Press
An Imprint of Wildside Press
Rockville, Maryland
MMV

WEST COAST STUDIES
ISSN 1041-4037
Number Five

Library of Congress Cataloging in Publication Data:

San Quentin : the evolution of a California state prison / edited by Bonnie L. Petry and Michael Burgess.
p. cm. — (West Coast studies, ISSN 1041-4037 ; no. 5)
Includes bibliographical references and index.
ISBN 0-89370-336-2 (cloth). — ISBN 0-89370-436-9 (pbk.)
1. California State Prison at San Quentin—History. 2. Prison administration—California—History. I. Petry, Bonnie L. (Bonnie Louise), 1957- . II. Burgess, Michael, 1948- . III. Series.
HV9475.C3S763 2005 97-40383
365/979462—dc21 CIP

Published in the United States of America
by The Borgo Press, an imprint of Wildside Press

FIRST EDITION

CONTENTS

DEDICATION

For Our Better Halves

INTRODUCTION

As of this writing it has been quite some time since a book on the history of San Quentin Prison has been published and even longer since some of the material presented here has been published in any form, if at all.

James H. Wilkins's "Evolution of a State Prison, Historical Narrative of the Ten Years from 1851 to 1861..." was previously published only once as a series of articles in the *San Francisco Bulletin* from June 13, 1918 through July 10, 1918. Mr. Wilkins knew several of the people who actually participated in San Quentin's early history and had access to a variety of associated documents.

Published here for the first time are two annotated bibliographies, one by Herman K. Spector, former Senior Librarian at San Quentin Prison, and an original compilation by the editor. Both include fiction, primarily by former inmates, as well as nonfiction.

As long as they have existed, prisons and prisoners have fascinated people, and San Quentin continues this tradition. It is hoped that both the general reader and the historian ill find this collection to be useful as well as interesting and intriguing.

—Bonnie L. Petry
Michael Burgess
San Bernardino, California
28 August 2004

ACKNOWLEDGMENTS

Thanks to Allan Adrian, for first suggesting that these texts be reprinted, and for supplying copies of same; and to Erin B. Rogers, for keyboarding parts of the manuscript.

I.

THE EVOLUTION OF A STATE PRISON

by

James Harold Wilkins

1.

HISTORICAL NARRATIVE OF THE TEN YEARS FROM 1851 TO 1861, DURING THE PERIOD WHEN THE CARE AND EMPLOYMENT OF CONVICTS WAS TURNED OVER TO LESSEES

No record remains of the early history of San Quentin Prison for the ten years ending February 21, 1861, during which period this institution, so rich in history, was under the management and control of a lessee. That is to say, no record remains at the prison itself. Whether to economize space or for other good and sufficient reasons, from time to time books have been committed to the flames, so that the investigator is apt to run into a blind alley in any avenue of research.

Only by searching through musty legislative annals and forgotten books of record in Marin County, together with documents placed in my hands through the courtesy of Mr. Bert Schlesinger and from the early recollections I have of first hand narratives from the lips of witnesses of the facts, have I been able to reconstruct the ancient institution into a recognizable shape.

For five years after the American occupation, California seems to have worried along without any fixed penal laws or penal institutions. Local jails were few and far between. Indeed, there were only six in the State prior to 1849, in the following towns: San Francisco, San Jose, Monterey, Santa Barbara, Los Angeles, and San Diego.

In the early gold rush, crossroads justice, administered by jurors chosen on the spot, seemed sufficient and effective. But when California became a State, the first session of the legislature, in 1850, passed a long act defining crime in general and its punishment. The list of criminal offenses embraced all the natural and recognized breaches of social law, known as felonies. But it was not a draconian code. Punishments imposed were remarkably light. For instance, bigamy was punishable by imprisonment for a term of not less than three months nor more than two years. The serious crime of arson, sometimes involving great destruction, was punishable by imprisonment from one to five years. Only in the case of larceny, when the value of the stolen goods exceeded the sum of $50, was the penalty extreme. At the discretion of the jury the punishment might be death. This was to reach those most abhorrent forms of crimes—horse or cattle stealing or robbing sluice boxes in the mining districts. A number of larcenists were actually executed before this bloodthirsty section of the act was repealed.

For the purposes of this act every county jail was declared to be a State prison until such time as the State should build one. Sheriffs were directed to work convicts on public account. If there were no suitable work in a particular county the Sheriff was empowered to transfer his "State convicts" to some other county, where their services were in greater demand.

This was, of course, only a stop gap proceeding. The law worked rather worse than expected. County jails filled up with a permanent and dangerous population. Gentlemen who had been guilty of no greater fault than cultivating a "souse," with a little disorderly conduct thrown in, were often compelled to "cell" overnight with a horse thief and a highwayman for mates, to the great scandal of the community.

Moreover, as the county jails were made of the most flimsy material, so that the more desperate and determined prisoners were able to escape pretty much at will, the presence of one of these institutions was a constant source of anxiety to the neighborhood.

Legislatures met every year at that period of the State's history. So in 1851 the whole question of securing a single and permanent location for a State prison was taken up and disposed of by legislation. The solution of the problem followed the line of least resistances—the old, old plan, always popular, but seldom successful, of getting something for nothing. For this purpose the act provided for the turning over of all convicts to lessees, who should clothe, feed, shelter, and guard them, construct cell buildings and other permanent works, receiving in return as compensation the free use of such convict labor not engaged in public work. In other words, the State proposed to run its prison for ten years without cost and receive something handsome in return.

By joint resolution Vallejo was named as the site for the new prison. M. G. Vallejo had leased the ground to the State, with an agreement to deed the same as soon as a State prison was erected thereon. He had also contracted to donate "125,000 in cash towards the erection of a State prison to be built of "dressed stone" of a design to be determined by the Commissioner of Public Buildings.

General Vallejo was booming the north end of the bay with great effect. He had already located the army headquarters at Benicia and made that port the terminal for the Pacific Mail steamships. And at this session of the Legislature the city of Vallejo was named as the permanent capital of the State and the home of all State institutions, dependent on the performance of a scheme of princely munificence on the part of General Vallejo. How the city of Vallejo lost the coveted prize and how Sacramento won it is of public interest, but no part of this story. How the site of the prison came to be shifted from Vallejo to San Quentin is.

Here is the text of the act, leaving out certain sections that would hardly concern the reader:

An Act Providing for Securing the State Prison Convicts Passed April 25, 1851

The People of the State of California, represented in Senate and Assembly, do enact as follows:

1. M. G. Vallejo and James M. Estell are hereby made the lessees of the prison, prison grounds of the State, and of all prisoners who are now in custody under sentence of imprisonment in the State Prison, and of all persons hereafter convicted in this State, who may be sentenced to imprisonment in the State Prison, by sentence of a competent court, or commutation by the Governor, during their terms of imprisonment, for the time upon the conditions hereinafter provided.
2. The said lessees, before entering upon their duties as provided in this act, shall file in the office of the Secretary of State, their bond in the penalty of one hundred thousand dollars, conditioned for the faithful performance of their duties as such lessees, and to hold the State free from every expense for the subsistence, clothing, security, and safekeeping of State Prison convicts, during the continuance of such lease. Such bond shall be given with at keast two sufficient sureties to be approved by the Governor. Upon filing such bond the Governor shall cause a notice of such fact to be published in as many public newspapers in the State as he may deem necessary. Such notice shall also contain the statement that M. G. Vallejo and James M. Estell have, by filing such bond, become the lessees as provided by this act.
3. Upon filing this bond, as aforesaid, in Section 2, the said Vallejo and Estell shall be considered the lessees, as provided in Section 1 of this Act, and shall continue as such lessees for the period of ten years from and after this Act. Said lessees shall thereupon immediately prepare suitable temporary buildings and secure prison ships, or vessels properly arranged for

the health and security of the convicts, until the State shall build the State prison. They shall provide food and clothing, medicine, and medical attendance for all convicts committed to the State Prison during the continuance of their lease, and shall also, during such time, provide all tools, chains, rings, and bolts necessary, and shall bear all the expenses of superintendents, assistants, officers, and guards employed in or about the prison, and all other expenses attending the keeping and maintenance of the prisoners.

4-5. These relate to the employment of an executive officer by the lessees with the title of superintendent, and the appointment of other officials and guards.

6. The Governor shall appoint, by and with the advice and consent of the Senate, three inspectors of the State Prison, who shall severally take the oath of office, which shall be filled in the office of the Secretary of State. Any two of the inspectors shall constitute a board to perform the duties of inspectors as provided in the next section.

7. The inspectors shall make all rules and regulations, which they may deem proper, for the discipline of the prison and not inconsistent with law, for the safekeeping, health, and cleanliness of the prisoners, copies of which they shall cause to be posted up in conspicuous parts of the prison and prison grounds. Provided, that this act shall not be so construed as to confine the labor of the prisoners within the walls of said prison, or to any particular place of labor.

8. Female prisoners shall not be employed in company with the male prisoners, but may be otherwise employed as the superintendent may direct, and said female prisoners shall be provided with separate and distinct buildings, and receive their food apart from the male prisoners.

9-12. These are not of general interest.

13. It shall be the duty of the Sheriff, of his deputy, of the different counties, immediately upon the receipt of

the clerk's certificate to proceed and deliver to the lessees or superintendent of the State Prison, all persons sentenced to imprisonment in said prison, upon the receipt of said lessees or superintendent, for which service the Sheriff or his deputy shall receive one dollar per mile for every prisoner taken by him for every mile actually traveled, in going from the place of conviction to the State Prison, which account shall be audited by the comptroller and paid by the Treasurer of the State out of any moneys not otherwise appropriated.

14. Whenever any prisoner or prisoners escape, it should be the duty of the lessees or superintendent to offer a reward not exceeding twenty-five hundred dollars for his or their apprehension and delivery to said prison, which reward so offered shall in no instance be chargeable to the State.

15-16 These exempt officers and guards from jury duty, and allow certain State officers to visit the prison at will.

As the casual reader will see, the act was very loosely drawn. In Section 7 it is distinctly provided that nothing in the act shall be so construed as to confine the labor of the prisoners within the walls of said prison, or to any particular place of labor. Following this clause, convicts were worked not only in Marin County, but elsewhere. Once, several convicts were sent to Mariposa County to prospect for a mythical gold mine. Only one guard was sent with four or five prisoners. The guard came back alone.

Another rather raw provision was allowing sheriffs one dollar for each mile traveled in transporting convicts to the State Prison. It certainly stimulated sheriffs to keep a sharp eye on possible material for transportation bills. In the old tabulated list of convicts still preserved, I have noticed names of Indians convicted of forgery in the early days, of whom it might be stated with certainty that they were unable to write their own names, not to speak of the names of others. Doubtless, on the advice of the sheriff, they were willing to plead guilty to any charge, and so materially increased the bulk of his bank roll.

The prison inspectors, on the other hand, were allowed neither salary nor expenses. Governor Bigler appointed as inspectors George McDougall, Horace W. Carpentier, and James Miller, who were duly confirmed. They were men of ability and character. I am in doubt whether James Miller was the well-known pioneer and landowner of Marin County or Senator James Miller of Mariposa. The above description would apply equally to either of them.

2.

SAN QUENTIN'S NATAL DAY AND THE FIRST SIX MONTHS OF ITS EXISTENCE AS A PENITENTIARY FOR THE INCARCERATION OF CRIMINALS

In the light of human experience it seems almost incredible that the framers of the act of 1851 seriously believed that for many years to come not more than fifty convicts would at the same time be confined under commitments for felony. Yet that such was the case is proved by a contemporary report of a legislative committee and other official documents. Such also was the firm belief of the lessees. They expected to have the free service of a small, compact body of men who could be profitably employed, easily guarded, and cheaply fed, who could be confined at night on a prison ship until such time as the State would build a prison at Vallejo as contemplated by the act.

For some reason the act of 1851 did not become effective until July 1 of the same year, when all prisoners then and thereafter convicted came under the jurisdiction of the lessees. Temporary arrangements for their maintenance were made with Colonel John C. Hays, Sheriff of San Francisco. I can find no record of the precise incident, but it is a fact referred to in many official documents that nearly the entire number, twenty-five all told, made their escape from Colonel Hays some time in the latter part of 1851. So the lessees had ample time to reconstruct an old hulk into a prison boat for the occupancy of future prisoners. Quite a few were housed therein by the beginning of the new year.

VALLEJO QUITS

In the meanwhile, plans had greatly changed. The legislature of 1852 practically revoked its former action relative to naming Vallejo as the State's capital, though legislature assembled there in 1853. All of M. G. Vallejo's dreams of a metropolis of public buildings and public institutions in the city bearing his name vanished forever. Under these circumstances, General Vallejo asked to be released from his position as lessee. This was granted by legislative act of 1852, and J. M. Estell, who was also a general, by the way, was declared the sole lessee, upon furnishing a new bond of $100,000 and making "proper settlement" with his late co-lessee. The bond was furnished and "proper settlement" presumably made.

At the same time, by an act passed May 1, 1852, the prison inspectors and the commissioner of public buildings were directed to select a suitable site for a State prison, "not to exceed 20 acres," and purchase the same at a price agreeable to the Governor. They were also empowered to let a contract for the construction of a prison building. It is known that the inspectors examined various promising locations, but finally selected Quentin Point as the most desirable. I should like to know who wished the "San" onto that Point. In all the early records and maps, that interesting bit of landscape was known as Quentin Point, and the great Spanish grant was entitled Rancho Punta de Quentín. There was a Saint Quentin—a very capable and enterprising saint—deserving any honor man might bestow. But the Point was not named after him, but from an Indian chief called Quentín, who had his headquarters at the point in early days. The early Americans had an impression that the word "San" or "Santa" ought to be prefixed to every Spanish name of a natural object. Many used to call the famous mountain San Diablo. I can account for the connection of "San" with

Quentin in no other way. It may be added here that the correct pronunciation is "Kaynteen."

What the Records Show

In *Book "A"* of Marin County Records can be found a deed from Benjamin R. Buckalew to James A. Graham, commissioner of public buildings, and to George McDougall, Horace W. Carpentier, and James Miller, as agents of John Bigler, Governor of California, and to his successors in office, conveying twenty acres of land at Quentin Point to be used in perpetuity as a State Prison. The description of the land is such that no surveyor could retrace the lines. The outline of the tract is, however, made evident by a map that accompanies it. In a general way it included, by due north, west, and south lines and the waters of the bay, what is now the immediate prison premises. The consideration was $10,000 and the date July 7, 1852.

Buckalew also made an independent contract with the State to connect a small rocky islet known as Agnes Island with the mainland and extend thence a wharf to deep water.

The State thus having secured a site for its prison, the hulk with its load of convicts was towed up the bay and moored under the shoulder of Quentin Point, nearly at the exact spot where the prison boat lands today. The date of its arrival was July 14, 1852, which may be considered as the penal institution's natal day. As far as I can gather from various sources, the number of convicts brought over on the hulk was between forty and fifty, not less than the former nor more than the latter. To this extent I can speak with certainty.

The first few months seem to have been spent in rush work on temporary quarters for officers, digging wells for a water supply and other enterprises essential for permanent occupation. No natural water or spring of any volume existed on the peninsula and the inspectors certainly took a long chance in locating a public institution in such an area of aridity. Sufficient water, however, was developed for domestic purposes by the exercise of the closest economy.

THEY LOST MONEY

It must be evident that so far the lessee had been up against a losing game. For more than a year he had been feeding, lodging and guarding a large number of prisoners. He had converted the old hulk into a floating Bastille at considerable expense. He had been under heavy expense for material of various kinds. And so far the account was entirely on one side of the ledger. General Estell was a man of means, but this sort of thing could not continue forever. Therefore, in order to reduce the monthly outgo he annexed several silent partners, who assumed a half interest in the profits and losses of the lease. The names of these partners were Ferdinand Vassault, Robert Allen, and Andrew Garr. All three men were well known figures in the past.

The first mention of these gentlemen appears in a deed from Benjamin R. Buckalew to James M. Estell, Ferdinand Vassault, Robert Allen, and Andrew Garr conveying a tract of sixteen acres, adjoining the previously described twenty-acre tract on the northwest. The deed recites that it shall be used as a "steam brickyard." Also, that the intent of the grantor was to convey a one-half interest to James M. Estell and one-half to the other grantees. The consideration was $5, or, in other words, the transfer was in the nature of a gift. In those days the true consideration was always named in a conveyance of real property.

The date of this deed was September 5, 1852. It em braced the property which was exploited for years by the brick-making enterprises of the prison. As is seen, it was entirely the property of the lessee. How it came into the ownership of the State is a very curious tangle which I might as well tell here, although it is anticipating the narrative.

SOLD TO STATE

Estell and his associates formed a corporation known as the San Francisco Manufacturing Company, Estell retaining half of the stock. The sixteen acres and the personal property of the individual members concerned in the lease was turned over to the corporation by deed dated September 22, 1853. On July 6, 1854, the land was transferred to Archibald Woods for a consideration of $30,150, at a time when it was the backbone of the prison industry. Archibald Woods deeded it to Governor Bigler on July 3, 1855, for a consideration of $40,000. The chain of title to the land leading up to the State seems complete as far as the records go. Yet in the final settlement with Estell by the State, it seems to have been admitted generally that either Estell owned the land or had a valid claim against the State for $48,000. It may be that Woods was only a dummy for Estell, and that the $40,000 consideration in the deed to Bigler was never paid by the State.

To resume the narrative, it was far too late in the fall to begin making brick and to lay the foundation of an income. In the meantime the fallibility of human judgment was being aptly illustrated. I have said that wise men of the State had forecast that there never would be more than fifty convicts confined at any one time for years and years to come. But almost from the moment that the lessee had moored his junk under the shoulder of Quentin Point, recruits to his interesting family began to flow in rapidly. Well before the end of the year the hundred mark was passed without any symptom of letting up. The hulk was filled to the limit of its capacity—even after crowding the men like sardines in a box. Sundry escapes helped a little, but not enough to afford permanent relief. The situation demanded the immediate construction of all buildings, which by the terms of the lessee were to be built at the State's expense, not by the lessee.

3.

HOW LEGISLATIVE QUARRELS DELAYED THE CONSTRUCTION OF MODERN PRISON BUILDINGS AS HORRORS OF THE OLD PRISON SHIP WERE MULTIPLIED

By an act referred to in the previous chapter, passed by the Legislature on May 1, 1852, the prison Directors had been authorized not only to select and purchase a suitable site for the prison (not to exceed twenty acres in extent), but also to prepare plans for the construction of necessary buildings and contract for the construction of the same, subject to the approval of the Governor. No limitation was placed on the price. The plans were prepared by the Commissioner of Public Buildings, Graham. On October 12, 1852, a contract was let to James M. Estell, Ferdinand Vassault, Robert Allen, and Andrew Garr, they being the lowest bidder. A copy of the contract is extant, but not the plans. It deals only in quantities—so much per square foot for masonry, so much per thousand for brick in place, so much per cubic yard for excavation. All that one can see with certainty is that it ran into big money, notwithstanding the fact that the contractors, who had the benefit of free labor, free quarries, and free brick works, were thus able to underbid other competitors. The plans seems to have included the Greek, Roman, Gothic, and Moorish types of architecture, for there are stray allusions to Doric columns, Roman towers, arches, and minuets.

By the original act of 1851, the inspectors were directed to report on or before January 28 of each year the condition of the institution under their care. The report rendered January 30, 1853, is still extant. It recites the labors of the inspectors to select a suitable site, that they had examined the "Island of Goates" and Angel Island, both of which were desirable but the title uncertain, that they had finally concluded that Point Quentin had more advantages than any other location, that in the further performance of their duties, they had let a contract for the construction of a modern prison, that the contractors were rapidly progressing on the work—had done most of the grading and were getting out building rock from quarries on their own land and on Marin Island. Owing to rapid increase of prisoners, for beyond previous calculations, it had been deemed expedient to build a prison large enough to house 250 inmates, which they deemed would exceed the largest number that would ever be suffering punishment at any one time. Temporary quarters for officers and guards had been constructed, also a general kitchen and convict dining room. The food was plentiful, well prepared, and of good quality. The average bill of fare appended would have an appetizing effect on the reader in these days of stern deprivation.

The living conditions on board the prison ship, wrote the inspectors, were bad; very bad. One hundred and fifty men were confined at night in quarters designated for a maximum of fifty. As a consequence, four men were locked up in a cell eight by eight feet. Notwithstanding the best efforts at ventilation, the air became so foul that only the most resolute and seasoned guards were able to descend into the hulk and unlock the prisoners in the morning. The health of the convicts was suffering in consequence, and there were no facilities, such as a hospital, to care for the sick. All of which was deplorable, but which would be remedied as soon as the first cell building was completed. In consequence of the open nature of the work, and the fact that the prisoners wore no distinguishing clothes, a number of escapes had been effected, and in pursuit of the fugitives some had been killed by the guards and some were still at large. Concerning this interesting phase of prison activities no further particulars were vouchsafed. When a man was dead in those days he was supposed to remain dead, and that terminated human interest in him.

Committees were appointed by both branches of the legislature which visited the prison and rendered widely divergent reports. The Senate committee was complimentary, praising the manner in which the lessee was struggling against enormous and unexpected difficulties; it patted the contractors on the back for their energy in rushing work on the prison buildings, and found no apparent ground for honest criticism.

It may be mentioned that Estell was a State Senator that year.

The Assembly committee's report on the other hand was a corker. It condemned the contract system in general, the lessee in particular, and especially denounced the inspectors for ordering the construction of the State Prison buildings at a cost ruinous in the extreme. Out of the disagreement a fierce legislative ruction was waged that finally ended in the passage of three radical acts.

New Act Passed

First, by the act of May 1, 1852, the prison inspectors were allowed $500 each year for personal expense. This was repealed.

Second, the contract entered into with the lessee in 1851 was declared null and void, and the entire organization of the State Prison at San Quentin changed to the bone. (It is here that the prefix "San" first appears in any official documents.) The institution was placed under the control and management of a board of prison commissioners, who were authorized to enter upon the property, appoint subordinate officers, purchase supplies, and exercise a general supervision over its affairs. The Board of Prison Commissioners named were R. M. Anderson, Lieutenant Governor of the State, G. W. Whitman, State Controller, and Henry Bates, State Treasurer, and their successors in office. No mention is made of compensation to the lessee for his very unproductive expenditure up to date. Nor does it appear that he had committed any breach of his contract that could make it voidable.

Third, the contract entered into by the Commissioner of Public Buildings with James M. Estell and others, was cancelled, as far as that could be accomplished by a legislative act. The State Prison Commissioners were directed to let a contract for a building sufficient to accommodate 250 prisoners, together with officer's quarters, at a cost not to exceed $135,000.

The new Prison Commissioners had the law, but Estell had the works. He cordially entertained the gentlemen when they appeared on the scene, but there his condescension ended. He informed them pleasantly that the legislature had no power whatever to cancel a contract arbitrarily; that such a power rested solely in the courts. He had the best legal advice obtainable on the subject, and moreover, he advised the Commissioners that he had not been born yesterday himself. Until further notice, he would recognize the authority of the prison inspectors, and nobody else.

So, two rival bodies struggled for mastery at San Quentin. The new commissioners stormed and talked of force to gain possession, but Estell was recognized as a man of courage and determination. Besides, he was backed up by twenty officers and guards, who, whatever may have been their shortcomings otherwise, were men of iron nerve. In calmly reviewing the facts, it is clear enough that a rather raw piece of injustice was attempted in the hostile legislation against Estell, for which no foundation seems to have been laid. Throughout, Governor Bigler played rather an ignoble part. The lease to Estell was mostly of his making. The Prison inspectors were Bigler's own appointees. Yet he was clearly afraid of the legislature and readily signed their plainly unfair measures. Throughout his career, the executive showed extreme dexterity in carrying water on both shoulders. As soon as the Legislature adjourned, he recognized the apparently ousted prison inspectors as legally constituted officers, and paid no attention whatever to the newly created Board of Prison Commissioners.

COMPLETE BUILDING

But the resultant confusion called a temporary halt in the construction of the contemplated prison buildings. The former contractors could not proceed with their work in the face of the certainty that their bills would be held up by the Controller and Treasurer, who were members of this hostile commission. That Commission itself advertised for bids for the construction of prison buildings, in conformity with the act limiting the expenditure of $135,000. They received bids all right, but as they were all conditioned on the elimination of Estell and his sidekicks, the proposals came to naught.

In the meantime, things were going from bad to worse. Nearly every day brought a fresh addition to the increasing convict family, and disease rapidly spread. During the summer of 1853, Estell engaged Dr. Alfred W. Taliaferro of San Rafael as prison physician, who paid daily visits to San Quentin and received from the lessee a salary of $200 a month. I have often heard this fine old Esculapian decant on the horrors of the prison ship. It was due to his urgency that a small frame hospital was constructed to care for the sick, and the crowded condition was in some measure relieved by allowing as many trusties as possible to sleep in temporary quarters on land.

In the meanwhile, during the official deadlock something had to be done. Having the stone, brick, and labor on hand, Estell proceeded to construct the first cell building at San Quentin. This was completed early in 1854, and is the first cell building to the left as you enter the prison by the front gate. Three stories are of stone, the last of brick. It is now referred to as the "Stone Building." For the payment of the same the lessee took a gambler's chance. In the fullness of time he received several payments, a total somewhat less than $75,000, which, with all things considered, was a low price for an extremely well built and serviceable structure.

4.

DARK DAYS FOR PRISON LESSEE AND AN INCIDENT THAT ILLUSTRATES TRIUMPH OF WRONG OVER RIGHT

It was not until June, 1853, that the lessee of San Quentin Prison received the first financial return from his investment in convict labor through the sale of the product of the "steam brickyard." Up to that time the financial going had been very bad. According to a statement of General Estell, he had invested nearly $200,000 in performing his side of the contract, with nothing to show but the plant, and that of unknown value. It was plain that the gentleman and his associates were feeling the pinch of poverty.

At this time the maintenance cost, including a large payroll, must have been $75,000 a year, not counting the cost of the first cell building, which was mainly constructed in 1853.

Even after productive labor began, it was no easy task to make both ends meet. The institution drifted along in a happy-go-lucky way. Sometimes it was a feast, sometimes a famine—dependent on the sale of a kiln of brick or an order for rock. Sometimes it was kindness, sometimes kicks—dependent on the disposition of the convicts to behave themselves or raise some novel kind of hell. While no general break took place during this period, escapes or attempts to escape were of almost daily occurrence. Some were recaptured and an uncertain number killed by the guards. From all that I can gather, General Estell was not a hardhearted man and inclined to greater leniency than most of his officers approved, as indicated by a joint request for higher wages and harsher discipline. I knew the General in later years. He did not impress me as a harsh taskmaster.

ANOTHER NAME

The cell building referred to in the last chapter was completed early in 1854. The ground floor was devoted to quarters for officers and guards and a general office. The tiers of cells above were sufficient to house 150 men, or more by doubling up. The prison ship thereafter disappears from history.

That "pull" exercised a potent sway in securing special favors for convicts can be seen in the following letter. The reader will also note that San Quentin Prison was also known then as "Corte Madera State Prison."

Corte Madera State Prison,
July 6, 1854

Judge Heydenfelt, Sir:

I deem it the most essential part of my duty to indite a few lines in order, if possible, to express my gratitude for the feeling interest you have manifested in me. But words have not coloring sufficient to paint the grateful emotion of the heart toward one whose kindly acts were elicited by the pure impulse of Christian feeling and charity. It is only now, when I contrast my situation with others, that I can fully comprehend and appreciate the value of your influence with General Estell. The civility with which I was treated, the indulgence conferred upon me, and all the great trust placed upon your honor, renders my obligations towards you and the general one hundredfold more obvious; and it shall be my continued prayer to God that no action of mine will subject me to become the vassal of misplaced confidence.

It would be utterly useless for me to attempt to describe the kindness and humility showed me by the generous General Estell. His reception of me was one which I can never forget and which a whole life of servitude would be inadequate to repay. He was on shore when my commitment was presented him, and desiring me to wait for him at the office, he there addressed me with all the feeling of a parent. He accepted my pledge of honor and placed no restrictions on my liberty, and gave orders that I should live at his hotel, outside the guards, and receive the same fare, after the officers, in the dining room. He also placed upon me the injunction that his liberality toward me should be avoided in my communication with friends, lest such indulgence should subject him to the censure of the community. What blessings are conferred upon the unfortunates whose luckless fate consigns them to the discipline of a State prison, to be placed under the benevolent guardiancy of such a humane gentleman as General Estell. He is always alive to every feeling of sympathy and consideration toward those who are placed under his charge; and it is only to be regretted that there are so many whose depraved natures are ever ready to take advantage of any indulgence which he offers and thereby involve him in difficulty. The superintendent, Mr. Tice, seems to be a perfect gentleman, and Mr. Gray, Captain Brouder, and Lieutenant Hays are declared to be without parallel; in fact, they seem to be everything that is desirable in officers.

You may easily infer that the change from county jail to the blessing I now possess is decidedly congenial and has been the means of alleviating in a great degree the oppression which bore so heavily on me. I shall therefore with all patience and humility and a continual feeling of gratitude abide the compassionate consideration of the Governor.

I shall keep a journal of events while in prison—the reminiscences may prove beneficial in after life.

And now all that is necessary to "cap the climax" of my comfort is a few plugs of common tobacco. I should regard the arrival of such a luxury as an indescribable favor, and should your kindness sanction this request, please direct the package direct to Mr. Tice,

Superintendent of State Prison, as there are almost daily arrival of boats from San Francisco.

I remain, kind sir, your very devoted, humble servant,

—Thos. McFarland Foley

After handing out this remarkable line of "bull," it may be interesting to follow up the career of Thomas McFarland Foley in order to see how he filled on his perfervid promises, and how long he continued to enjoy the blessings of a residence at Corte Madera State Prison, under the humanizing influence of General Estell, whose name he misspelled so often [as Estill] in the above letter.

Robbed the Safe

Either to further oblige his friend, Judge Heydenfelt, or because Thomas McFarland Foley succeeded in impressing Estell with the idea of his absolute fidelity to himself, it is certain that three weeks after his arrival that this prisoner was actually appointed a night guard on a salary. What happened was in the familiar line that has saddened so many of us with world experience—the apparent triumph of wrong over right. The prisoner-guard speedily became accustomed to his surroundings, particularly with the location of the key to the safe. Two months after writing his letter of July 6, or, to be exact, on the night of September 11, 1854, he burglarized the prison safe, secured somewhat over $500 of poor Estell's money, and faded away.

In place of the money, he left a long and carefully prepared letter to the lessee, written in the same extravaganza style as the letter to Judge Heydenfelt, in which he expressed a sincere and lasting regret that the General might perhaps interpret his sudden leave-taking as an act of ingratitude. But he wished to assure the lessee that recent events of a compelling nature made his further stay at the prison impracticable. As to the trifling pecuniary obligation, which he trusted his kind friend would regard as inconsiderable, he wished to assure General Estell that he would always regard it as a debt of honor, and that he would hasten to repay it at the earliest convenient moment.

I have stated that Estell was not a hardhearted man, but I tremble to think what would have happened to Thomas McFarland Foley if the general had ever laid his hands on him. All the State was diligently combed for him, but his getaway was complete.

Indeed, it was the wide extension of the "trusty" system that was largely responsible for the great number of escapes. Once the fugitives reached what were then the wooded fastnesses of Marin, they were practically safe from pursuit. Thence they descended on the simple-minded farmers, and sometimes added the outrage of women to mere depredations for food. Many also escaped from guards when employed at some distance from the prison, while cutting wood for the brickyard or engaged in various other occupations, principally connected with prison economics. Against this serious state of affairs the Marinites, through their Grand Jury, bawled lustily, but bawled in vain.

5.

PEACE OFFICERS IN THE PIONEER DAYS MADE HANDSOME PROFITS IN TRANSPORTING CRIMINALS TO THE PENITENTIARY AND IN OTHER WAYS WHEN THE OPPORTUNITY OFFERED

That the criminal element was not without profit to the peace officer in the olden days was indicated by the fact that he received a fee of $1 a mile for each mile traveled in transporting a prisoner from a given county seat to the penitentiary. Moreover, the official distances for measuring mileage are much shorter now than they used to be. The State seems to have shrunk materially with age. For instance the official distance from Los Angeles to San Quentin Prison, as fixed by statute passed in 1852, measured by the sea route, presumably, was 660 miles. Perhaps the modern geographies are wrong.

As everything went by fees—so much for an arrest, and so much for bringing a prisoner into court—a few enterprising prisoners were a real godsend to a sheriff's office. Some profits were not so legitimate. Nearly everybody at that time carried considerable money on their persons, or its equivalent—[gold] dust. Many parties who passed through officer's hands complained bitterly that the assets taken from them at the time of their arrests had diminished sadly when they were returned. Here is a case in point:

William Hamilton Hawkins, a Negro, was received in San Quentin Prison, as will be seen, by the accompanying correspondence. He had been an enterprising burglar and expert jail breaker, and had amassed considerable wealth. In fact, he was evidently preparing to retire from business, as he had a large sum in drafts on New York in his possession when arrested at Monterey. When he arrived at San Quentin, it was found that the prisoner's property had been retained by the Sheriff of Monterey. As Estell was under heavy bond, as custodian of convict property, he naturally made a demand on the sheriff, backed by an order from Hawkins. The following documents are self explanatory:

Hawkins' Order

California State Prison, August 20, 1853
Mr. Roach, Sheriff of Monterey County, California

Sir:

Please deliver to J. M. Estell, lesee of the State Prison of California, or order, a draft for three hundred dollars drawn by Adams & Co. in favor of William Hamilton payable in New York. Also one draft drawn by Adams & Co. for six hundred dollars in favor of William Hamilton. Also, one draft drawn by Wells,

Fargo Company for one thousand dollars in favor of William Hamilton. Also, one draft drawn by Wells, Fargo Co., for one thousand, one hundred dollars in favor of William H. Hamilton, there being a duplicate of each draft. Also, about three hundred and thirty dollars in coin. Also, three hundred dollars worth of specimens. Also, one carpet bag, containing three shirts, one pair plaid pants, one gray cloth vest, one pair of shoes and small revolver; being all and singular the property taken from me when I was arrested at Monterey.

—William Hamilton Hawkins
Attest: J. M. Thompson
Capt. Guard, California State Prison

Estell's Demand

San Francisco, August 22, 1853
William Roach, Esq., Sheriff of Monterey

Sir:

I am informed by John McDougal and others that effects belonging to a State prisoner, William H. Hawkins, are left in your possession. Captain Thompson, superintendent of the prison, also informed me that the deputy sheriff of your county gave him the same information. The law makes it my duty to take in charge all the effects belonging to all State prisoners, holding it subject to the action of the State Prison inspectors. They also require of me a bond, with security in the sum of one hundred thousand dollars, to perform this duty faithfully.

The prisoner gave me an order for them for fear there might be some mistake concerning it.

I called on Wells, Fargo & Company and Adams & Company, and had the drafts cancelled on yesterday at the request of the prisoner and by order of the State inspectors.

I am happy to hear that you had sent word to me by the deputy that the effects are subject to my order, but I regret that they were not sent along with him.

Please deliver all the articles in your possession belonging to the prisoner to Captain Hunt, who will deliver them to me without compelling me to make the trip myself. I am truly yours,

—J. M. Estell,
Lessee, State Prison, California

Gets Love Song

Monterey, September 8, 1853

Received of William Roach, sheriff of Monterey, a part bag of placer specimens, and specimen pins, a love song, bead purse, and small bottle of Otto of Roses, with a few one dollar gold pieces; also a counterfeit five dollar California gold piece.

—James M. Hunt

As will be noticed, no mention is made of the drafts or of the considerable sum of money, except the few one dollar gold pieces and the counterfeit five dollar piece. The "love song" and the "small bottle of 'Otto of Roses'," not mentioned in the original order, were not considered a just and sufficient equivalent. Therefore, General Estell wrote a rather peppery letter to Sheriff Roach. That gentleman countered with an affidavit by his under-sheriff which seems intended to pass the buck in the direction of Captain Hunt. The affidavit follows:

TESTIMONY OF THOS. K. MONK

Thos. K. Monk, sworn:

I reside in Monterey; I was the undersheriff of Monterey at the time Hawkins, a convict, who had escaped from the State Prison, was arrested at that place; he was placed in my charge as sheriff; I stripped him and found a large quantity of small gold coin, some two or three hundred dollars' worth, and some six to eight thousand dollars in drafts (first of exchange), some on Adams & Co., and some on Wells Fargo & Co.; they were made payable in New York to his own order. I also found upon him various other articles of value, such as specimen breast pins, lockets. Captain Hunt of the *Major Tompkins* came to Monterey and brought some kind of written authority from General Estell and took his receipt for them; I filed away the receipt and letter or written authority in the sheriff's office of Monterey, so I think they are there yet; they were there when I left Monterey; I have been away since December last. At the time Hawkins was brought back to prison, a man by the name of Reynolds was deputized to bring him, and did so; it was the next trip of the steamer *Tompkins* (about a week after) that Captain Hunt brought the written authority to get the money, etc. I had given them to William Roach, the sheriff; he took them out to his house; and I sent for them when the written authority came, and they

> were sent; and I handed everything over to Captain Hunt. The money and jewelry were in leather bags; I did not then count the money, but it appeared to be all right. I have no doubt but the bags and drafts and everything remained when I handed them to Captain Hunt, just as they were when I took them from Hawkins. Hawkins was a black fellow.
>
> —Thos. K. Monk

Even this did not seem to satisfy Estell. More correspondence followed of a tropical character, but while the discussion was at fever heat, Hawkins generously poured oil upon the troubled waters by escaping for the third and last time. He never appeared again in the criminal annals of California, though there is reason to believe that he stayed long enough to win another stake. Years afterwards he was known to be living in New York, where he was reputed to be a man of property, and enjoyed an enviable social reputation.

6.

IN 1854 THE ESCAPE OF CONVICTS BECAME SO FREQUENT THAT THE PEOPLE IN NEIGHBORING COUNTIES WERE TERRORIZED BY DEPREDATIONS AND THREATENING CONDUCT

The year 1854 was, par excellence, the year of escapes at San Quentin Prison. Excepting the escape of twenty-five prisoners from Sheriff John C. Hays of San Francisco, while he was boarding them for the lessee, none appear to have taken French leave except by individual effort. But in the year above mentioned, at least four desperate and successful breaks occurred. The details are extremely imperfect, even the exact dates in some cases. On a foggy night on May 6, 1854, four prisoners cut their way through the roof of the new prison, overpowered and gagged the sole guard stationed there, made their way to *terra firma*, and vanished into the night.

On July 24 twelve convicts seized a small vessel at Sheppard's Cove immediately east of the prison, and made good their escape. Several, however, seemed to have been killed in this outbreak.

At an unknown date, some time in September, 1854, quite a formidable break occurred about a mile west of the prison, where two persons owned a brickyard. Fourteen convicts were passing this point, presumably on a wood cutting expedition, when they suddenly turned on their guards and a desperate conflict followed. Apparently the prisoners must have been armed, for the account states that several guards were killed and most of the prisoners, but that a few of the latter seized a whale boat owned by the brickyard, and made good their escape. All we know with certainty concerning this break is contained in a casual reference to it by General Estell in a report to an investigating committee. Purely to illustrate the heavy and unexpected expenditures to which he was subjected as lessee, he states that he had been compelled to buy the brickyard in order to eliminate so fruitful a source of escape.

GUARDS KILLED

On the night of December 27, 1854, a very serious break occurred among the prisoners working on the Marin Island stone quarry. The convicts rose en masse, killing several guards, and several of the belligerents were killed themselves. "Several" seems to have been a sufficiently comprehensive and definite word in all reports of casualties. No light whatever is thrown on the names or numbers of the slain. However, this much is clear, that after some extremely bitter fighting, the convicts were masters of the situation, and twenty-two sailed away for Contra Costa County. "Several" appear to have been killed by pursuing posses. Six were captured and lodged in Santa Clara County jail, where they effected a second escape two days later.

In the meanwhile, single-handed jail breakers were not inactive. In the record it appears that eighty-three convicts made their escape during the year 1854. It is known positively that those engaged in the two big escapes—from Sheppard's Cove and Marin Island—thirty-seven in all, landed in Contra Costa County. It is fair to presume that the surviving convicts who seized the schooner at the brickyard west of the prison reached the same destination. That leaves a balance of approximately fifty prisoners who distributed themselves about equally over the wooded sections of Marin County. There, through the long summer weather, they enjoyed themselves in contemplation of the beauties of nature, musing on the brook that babbled by, meanwhile trapping quail, pursuing the agile trout for food, and levying a sort of surtax on the farmer for such luxuries as blankets, butter, eggs, bacon, and kitchen utensils. No prince ever sat down to a more sumptuous table. Sometimes they traveled over the country in bands large enough to command fear, if not respect.

Farmers Take Part

It was quite an idyllic life. The boys lived on the fat of the land, and a kindly nature or an unkindly farmer honored every demand. General Estell admitted, in writing, that whenever a convict reached the brush, the case was hopeless, worse than exploring a haystack for a needle. So the escaped convict had little to fear from pursuit. Sometimes angry farmers formed posses and assumed the role of sleuths. But rubes are only dangerous while their Irish is up. They lack continuity of action. All the escaped prisoner had to do was to lay low for a day or so, until the rubes wearied of the manhunt and went home.

In a report of the Marin County Grand Jury during the month of January, 1854, the statement is made that to the best of public information not less than seventy-five escaped convicts were sojourning in Marin County, making the lives of the agrarian burdensome and terrifying women and children. The story is told in a rough, masculine way that gives it credence.

It is only fair to the lessee to hear his side of the story. I have selected the following salient features of a statement made by him for public consumption and later presented to the legislature:

> Since the first of January, 1851, ninety-eight convicts have escaped. Of this number forty-one have been recaptured. (This does not agree with the discharge list, which shows 153 escapes.)
>
> Quite a number have been killed in attempt to suppress revolts, and in efforts to retake those who had escaped. Only twenty-one, however, have been reported to the lessee.
>
> Over $12,000 have been paid for expenses and rewards for the return of escaped State Prison convicts.
>
> The prisoners have been employed, mostly, in making bricks and quarrying stone. Most of the mechanical branches are followed to a limited extent, but the want of buildings for shops and a wall to confine the mechanics who would be compelled to handle such tools as they could use in attempts to escape, has prevented the superintendent from following this plan. Indeed, the danger is so imminent that many who could be worked to the greatest advantage and profit have now to be kept chained in the cells in order to keep them safely. Guards could not be procured without this precaution.
>
> **Many Are Killed**
>
> Notwithstanding, I regret to be compelled to say, many *émeutes* have occurred during

the last year, all of which have been attended with loss of life. A number of convicts have been killed and wounded in these outbreaks and in all efforts to recapture them. This I deeply regret, but as it is, lives aside, I cannot hesitate to give the order to enforce obedience at every hazard. I feel it due to myself to refer to some of the facts in connection with the original lease under the law passed April 25, 1851.

At the time this contract was made, it was not contemplated that there would be [anything] to exceed fifty prisoners at any one time, for many years to come. This number, it was believed, could be safely kept in a prison ship, or "in temporary buildings, until such time as the State could build the State Prison." Instead of fifty, there are, this day, over three hundred, and if a safe prison with secure walls had been erected, so that the people of the different counties had the conviction that the proper punishment for crime would have been administered, mob law would not so readily have been resorted to, and the number at this day, I doubt not, would have reached five hundred. As it is, if all who were sent here could have been kept, the statistics show there would have been much over four hundred now.

New Wing Ordered

When it was found that the number was increasing so rapidly, the State, in obedience to the third section of the act referred to, ordered the building of one wing of the State Prison. This wing contains forty-eight cells, capable of containing four prisoners each. There is one large room below, capable of holding one hundred, but without a division. This room of course, if broken, would allow the whole number to escape.

Thus situated, we are in most imminent danger.

I have the mortification daily of seeing the graves of my brave guards, murdered by the hands of infamy, and meeting others maimed for life whilst in the discharge of their unenviable duty.

The California State Prison is an isolated building, standing in the center of twenty acres of land, without guard rooms, officers' quarters, infirmary or hospital rooms, and without even a kitchen.

The cells are there for holding the prisoners, and they are very safe. But the prisoners have to be marched three or four hundred yards for the purpose of obtaining their meals and for the performance of labor. Thus, an opportunity for a revolt is offered three times each day, while the whole of the prisoners (nearly three hundred) is embodied.

Wise men who have never been at the State Prison, but who know all about it through the newspapers, can tell [me] how to prevent escapes and outbreaks. I have conversed with hundreds and have listened patiently to hear something new. Truth compels me to say that no two of them have agreed in their views, and some of their pleas have been so palpably absurd that I could scarcely suppress a smile.

The prison is so situated that boats are necessarily compelled to come to and pass near it.

Two gentlemen of San Francisco owned a brickyard adjoining that of the State Prison. They had a right to and did keep such boats as they pleased. In a general revolt, fourteen of the prisoners took a whaleboat belonging to them and attempted to escape. Many of them were killed and wounded and guards were killed in the fight for the boat, but several escaped in it. On other occasions similiar occurrences happened with similiar results.

Buys Brickyard

Wise men tell me how to avoid such an occurrence, but I cannot learn of them. The gentlemen had a perfect right to own and occupy the property, to ship bricks, to own and keep such boats as they liked, and I had no legal right to control them. They intended to do no wrong, for they are both reputed to be as honorable men as there are in the State. I could not ask them to abandon their property on account of the State Prison, and the only thing I could do was to buy them out, which I did.

Dense fogs prevail for five months in the year. The Pacific Ocean is but a few miles westward of the prison, washing the base of the mountains beyond Corte Madera. Heavy winds lift dense fogs over the summit of the mountains, and precipitate them, without notice, on the eastern slope, rendering it impossible to distinguish an object a few yards off. Prisoners learn all the peculiarities of the location and are not slow in availing themselves of every opportunity that occurs.

Not a few have escaped by this means. It frequently happens that several days will elapse without the possibility of taking the prisoners from their cells in consequence of heavy fogs. On one occasion the prisoners passed an entire week in the cells without being able even to go to their meals, the fog being so dense during the time, that the lessee would not risk them out of the prison.

During these fogs, the powder and caps are all damp and the guns as well, all of which is well known to the convicts as to the guards. Consequently there is, at such times, greater danger of an *émeute*.

—J. M. Estell

7.

STORIES OF IRREGULARITIES AT THE PRISON CAUSED THE GOVERNOR TO ORDER AN INVESTIGATION, AND THE STORIES OF THE FEMALE PRISONERS READ LIKE BOCCACCIO

As a result of the escapes at San Quentin Prison during 1854, and because of the stories of irregularities that had aroused public opinion, Governor Bigler called on the prison inspectors and the Legislature to conduct a rigid investigation. The finding of the inspectors was embodied in their annual report. It found that the principal cause of escape was due to the extensive practice of the trusty system. It referred to the previous revolts and another, not mentioned elsewhere, which took place last year (1854) at the redwoods of Corte Madera, where a body of prisoners had been sent for wood, in which "several" of the guards were killed and "several" prisoners escaped. They lamented that, "having no authority to administer oaths or to require information by compulsory process, they had been obliged to rely on their own observation, together with such information as might be volunteered by the lessee and the questionable declarations of the prisoners themselves; that, while the number of prisoners reported to be killed in repeated insurrections was only twelve, the inspectors had reason to believe, on information deemed reliable, that much more than double that number have been killed and their names not reported, for fear of trouble and the expense of legal investigation."

While admitting the right of the lessee to employ prisoners at a distance from the prison establishment under the peculiar wording of the act of 1852, they insisted on such modification of the law as would confine convicts strictly to the prison territory.

Valuable Document

The report of the inspectors is too long to be printed here. It goes into the general subject of penology in a spirit of broad humility, far ahead of the age, and is a well-written public document.

The assembly appointed a special committee which sat at San Francisco and San Quentin for more than two weeks and gathered a large mass of testimony. Most of it came from discharged officers and guards of the prison, representing in large measure the gossip common around such an institution. Internal evidence indicates that much of it is highly colored with prejudice, but no one can fail to be convinced of certain serious facts:

1. That bars were, from time to time, maintained within the prison lines, to which prisoners had free access, though never in a State building proper. One of these was kept on board the prison ship, and at a later date one was kept in the cook house during the cell building construction of 1853.

2. That officers and guards, while personally brave, as the record of their slaughter in resisting outbreaks abundantly proves, were often addicted to drink and were guilty of serious breaches of discipline while under the influence of liquor.

3. That the trusty system had been carried to such an extent that unguarded convicts were permitted to roam more or less at will over Marin County and

were frequently sent to San Francisco on various errands, where they sometimes remained for days.

4. That the food supplied was generally of excellent quality, but at times irregular, due to financial pressure on the trustee.

5. That the private management of the prison was a failure, and that the condition of the prison without a wall or sufficient cell buildings to confine convicts in at night was a menace to society.

6. That the value of property in Marin County had greatly depreciated because of the location of the prison there and the continued escape of its desperate inmates.

Female Prisoners

Three female prisoners had been confined at the prison for various terms. They had been known familiarly and affectionately as Scotch Mary, Dolores, and Russian Kate. It is like taking a page out of Boccaccio to follow the tender amours of these unfortunate fairies, for such they must have been from all accounts. Though sequestered from the world, they had no reason to lament the absence of male admiration, so dear to ladies' hearts. Great jealousy existed between suitors for their favor. Two high officers, according to evidence, carried guns for each other over the question as to which should have the honor of being known as Scotch Mary's man. Dolores and Russian Kate were also charmers of the first order. It is quite unnecessary to relate the details of the squalid stories told under the sanctity of an oath concerning the women convicts. Some of them bear the strong earmarks of fabrication. But I can more readily credit the general charge from the fact that for more than a quarter of a century after the State had taken over the prison from the lessee, while the female convicts were still in the exclusive hands of male keepers, the same relation prevailed. Of this I have official knowledge to this extent that I have voted as

Prison Director to allow female prisoners to be taken outside the walls during the period of childbirth and for a reasonable time thereafter. I have talked with some of these unfortunate women but they resolutely refused, perhaps for prudential reasons, to fix the responsibility for their condition.

It was not until a prison matron was appointed that recurrent scandals ceased.

It might be added, all female prisoners had been discharged by the latter part of 1854. Scotch Mary, Dolores, and Russian Kate became only fragrant memories of the past.

A Hostile Witness

But to return to the prison investigation, I will select only the testimony that appears to me worthy of credence, and which, moreover will seem to give something of a picture of the condition that existed in what I might be permitted to term paradoxically the near but far distant past.

I will select as a curtain raiser the evidence of A. Jackson Tice, former superintendent. Guess what the "A." of his name stood for. He was a hostile witness, I presume, for he had recently lost a good job at the prison. Still, I think his statements are truthful. In the following affidavit we again meet our old friend, Thomas McFarland Foley.

A. Jackson Tice, sworn, says:

> I reside in San Francisco; I was employed as superintendent of the State prison from May 17, 1854, to some time in the latter part of July; I went back again and was about there a short time afterwards. I received instructions, both verbal and written, relative to the treatment of convicts. Gardner was put in for manslaughter July, 1854; General Estell wrote me that Gardner was a gentleman, and I must not put him in a cell or keep him to work, until he came up; I locked him up in the large room at the prison, in the basement

story, as long as I stayed there; I have understood he is escaped since I left there.

A man [was] sentenced for killing the editor of the *Police Gazette* in San Francisco; General Estell told me he wanted him to have all the liberties of the place and instructed me not to keep him confined; he said he did not want the guard to know that he was a prisoner; his name was Thomas McFarland Foley; his name is not on the book that I know of; General Estell was there when Foley was brought over; while he was there I went and locked up the other prisoners towards night, and General Estell took Foley into my office and talked with him. Estell said Foley was a perfect gentleman; that he had a letter from a friend of his; he is well educated, and never ought to have been convicted, and he thought he would be pardoned in a short time; he wished me to give him full liberties of the ground and to allow him to pass in and out, at his own convenience; also to allow him to sleep at the house, to furnish him with pen, ink, and paper, and also to allow him to eat with Judge Gates; Gates was a trusty convict who acted as steward at the house and had his liberty, and did not eat with the rest of the prisoners. About two weeks after, General Estell appointed Foley on night guard; he told me that he had made a night guard of Foley, that he was to oversee the grounds at night; I have understood he afterwards escaped while on night guard and left a note, stating that he would send $500 back that he took from the safe.

There was a convict named Brown who acted as clerk in the office while I was there; I think he was in for five years; I saw him here in town after I left the prison; his time had not expired; he came to my place of business on Liedesorff Street and showed me a petition he was circulating for his pardon; I signed it; he said that the General told him he might come and stay two or three days to get his friends to sign his petition; while he was here he forged a check on Macondray & Co., and was sentenced for ten years more, instead of obtaining a pardon.

8.

LEGISLATIVE INVESTIGATION SHOWED THAT PRISON FINANCES WERE IN A DEPLORABLE CONDITION, WHILE THE GUARDS AND PRISONERS WERE GIVEN TO EXCESSIVE DRINKING AT THE BAR

The testimony given before the legislative investigating committee exhibited, among other things, the deplorable state of the finances under the Estell lease. It will be remembered that shortly after the prison ship tied up at Quentin Point, the lessee joined in a partnership, in which he retained a half interest, his associates being Ferdinand Vassault, Robert Allen, and Andrew Garr, all of them men of wealth. Later the business was incorporated under the name of the San Francisco Mercantile Company. After a dismal year of financing, Ferdinand Vassault pocketed his loss like a cheerful loser and gaily retired. He was a man of pleasure in the old days, a *bon-vivant* and entertainer, whose varied and versatile gift of telling salacious stories made him deservedly popular in Bohemian society. Whatever induced him to engage in such an enterprise was a mystery to his admiring friends. Robert Allen and Andrew Garr held on for fully two years, when the San Francisco Mercantile Company finally disbanded. Doubtless Estell, too, would have abandoned the sinking ship, but he was tied on by a good and sufficient bond to the State in the sum of $200,000.

On the witness stand Allen stated that his personal loss amounted to $50,000, that of Andrew Garr the same, and that of Ferdinand Vassault half as much. Estell placed his personal loss at $127,000 although since the retirement of his partners he had cleared $45,000 by a lucky contract to supply rock and brick for the construction of the S.F. Custom House. Allen claimed the losses had accrued from the great and unexpected number of prisoners forced upon them, from bad management, from the gross overfeeding of prisoners, who received twice the ration allowed by the U.S. Army, and lastly, to direct peculation on the part of the officers of the San Francisco Mercantile Company, according to which the net loss had slightly exceeded a quarter of a million dollars.

Residents of Marin County gave cumulative evidence of the reign of terror that gripped that community by reason of the large number of escaped convicts who occupied dug-outs in the inaccessible mountain region, committing, as occasion served, many acts of banditry on the peaceful inhabitants. They testified, moreover, that valuable land had become absolutely unsalable by reason of the proximity of the State Prison.

Testimony Given

The following extracts from testimony given before the Assembly investigating committee size up the situation at its worst:

Deposition of Henry Hayes:

> I reside in San Francisco; I was employed as guard at the State Prison from November 25, 1852, until the third or fourth of November, 1854, and I have frequently been at the prison ever since—about every week; when I first went there, I think there were eighty-seven prisoners; there were ten men employed as guards, besides the captain of the guard; sometime in August last, Thomas

Ashton and Colonel Harper, both prisoners, were given arms and sent out on guard or on "the lookout" as they call it; Burns, one of the guard, and some others, had pre-emption claims in the neighborhood of Corte Madera, and they were in the habit of taking prisoners over to work on the claims; these claims were from two to four miles from the prison.

I have seen prisoners here in the city occasionally who had come over as cooks or sailors; it was generally when they had but a short time to stay; four was the largest number of convicts that I ever knew to come at once on any one vessel; that was in a small boat sent to the city after powder; they had one guard with them; they were not chained. The sick are generally well taken care of. There are only two guards on duty at a time in the night, one on the balcony and one on top of the prison building; no lights on the outside in the night. Many prisoners escaped at one time from the long room in the lower part of the prison; they pried the bars or grates [open] on one side, and escaped through the window; at another time four escaped through the top of the roof. They had an auger, and bored through the plank.

Mr. Gates, a convict, is permitted to sleep at the cookhouse, and one Chinaman; there is one of the guard sleeps there, but he did not stay up all night. General Gates is universally admitted to be a trusty-convict. The general opinion of the guard is that General Estell is not too cruel to convicts, but that he is too lenient with them.

ANOTHER WITNESS

Deposition of E. Buckley:

I reside in San Francisco; I was at the prison, as foreman of the prison building, from the 22nd day of August, 1854, to December of the same year; the management of the prisoners was very bad; convicts were frequently out shooting birds and out in boats without a guard; they were out fishing. A man by the name of Jackson and one by the name of Francis used to go out often; the latter has since escaped; there were female convicts; Mary Ann Wilson (Scotch Mary) used to do washing for money and spend the money at the bar on the prison grounds for liquor. I have frequently seen prisoners go to the bar and drink, and I have seen seven or eight at a time drinking at the bar; I have seen Mr. Gray, the lieutenant of the guard, order liquor to be given to the prisoners; I have seen Gray so drunk he could not walk straight, and he was led by one of the guard; his clothes, on one side, were muddy, as if he had been down.

Testimony of Peter Joyce:

I have seen Thompson, captain of the guard drunk; also Lieutenant Gray. I have seen a convict woman named Mary get very drunk, and the convict women were allowed to pass the guards to get liquor at Parker's Tavern, near Shephard's brickyard; a Negro convict also had the liberty to pass to bring liquor from the same place. I have seen convicts drunk and fighting with the mason who built the prison; they got their liquor at the bar which was kept at the mason's boarding house near the brickyard, and tended by Woods, one of the guards. I was instructed to let some convicts pass to get liquor. I had stopped them, but was told not to stop them. As soon as the masons had finished the prison, Woods' bar was discontinued and another bar started by Estes, captain of the guard, on board the prison brig. I once obtained from him a bottle of grog to give it to a band of prisoners sent with me to fetch wood. I understand that other guards were in the habit of doing the same thing. The liquor I gave to the prisoners was charged to me by my order, and when I presented my bill to the company for liquor thus furnished, the agents refused to pay it.

The prisoners were ordered out to work about daylight and were turned in about sunset. Sometimes on Sundays convicts were set at quarrying stone, loading brick and stone, burning brick, and such other work as was usually done on work days. Several prisoners went on Sundays to work on Capt. Thompson's ranch, where vegetables were raised for the use of the guards. On such occasions they usually received liquor, and came in from their work sometimes intoxicated; this was a common occurrence during the spring. The work done about the prison grounds on Sunday was usually done for the purpose of dispatch, to get off some scow or vessel. I have no prejudices or ill-feeling towards Mr. Estell; he has paid me every dollar he ever owed me.

PEOPLE AFRAID

Testimony of J. L. Van Reynegon:

I formerly resided in Marin County, about three miles from the prison; I have frequently seen convicts three or four miles from the prison grounds getting wood; they usually had one guard to each lighter or boat, from four to ten prisoners with each boat. The people of Marin are constantly in fear of prisoners, constantly expecting outbreaks; I have known many persons to object to living or settling there with families on account of the constant fear of outbreaks and violence of convicts. I offered my place for sale, and men objected to buying it on account of its proximity to the State Prison. I have a family and dreaded to leave my house, for fear of violence to my wife and daughter by escaped convicts; they are frequently making their escape; I have known a great number at a time lurking about and secreting themselves in the bushes; they lay about there and get plenty of game until their hair grows out; I have seen convicts that they called trustees in this city; they were allowed to go all over the city without a guard; one in particular.

Testimony of Joseph B. Wing:

I reside in San Francisco; am a police officer; I was employed as guard and overseer at Prison from January, 1853, to November of the same year; the female convicts were kept a portion of the time in the cabin on the prison brig, afterwards they were removed to a house (called the middle house), where Mr. Gray slept; there were four female convicts some of the time and three some of the time; no other man but Gray slept there after the women went there; the women were employed washing for the officers; sometimes one or more male convicts assisted them in bringing water and clothes or putting up clothes lines; the females eat apart from the male prisoners; I have known convict labor to be done on Sunday that was not necessary to save the property.

I was discharged from the guard. I did not agree very well with Judge Thompson, and I always supposed I was discharged on that account, but I never could find out; after I had been discharged, General Estell said I could go back again if I wanted to, whenever there should be a vacancy; I never got drunk at the prison; I might have got corned sometimes off duty, on the Fourth of July, or some such occasions; in 1853 there was a committee of the Legislature came there and after they left all the officers and guards got pretty tight. The reason why they got tight at that particular time was that there was plenty of liquor there; I suppose it was brought there on the account of the legislative committee being there; I have no prejudice or ill feeling towards General Estell; it would be unreasonable in me to have, for I have no reason to have; he always treated me well, for aught that I know. I disliked Captain Thompson; I had some difficulty with him; he got tight on one occasion and I told Major Daniels of it and that was the cause of the difficulty.

9.

STATE DRIVES HARD BARGAIN WITH ESTELL WHEN HE IS COMPELLED TO RELINQUISH CONTROL OF SAN QUENTIN BECAUSE OF THE INSUFFICIENT FACILITIES TO HOUSE CONVICTS

The first regularly appointed physician of San Quentin was Dr. Alfred W. Taliaferro. The name, through some perversity of linguistics, is pronounced as if spelled Toliver. He came to California with Lord Chas. S. Fairfax and others, forming what was known historically as the Virginia Colony. Fairfax and Taliaferro were fast friends, and when the former settled on the picturesque spot in Marin County that still bears his name, the latter joined him in this retreat and lived there for many years. From the time that the prison brig was moored at Quentin Point, he was a casual attendant on the sick. In August, 1853, Estell appointed him as regular physician of the prison at a salary of $200 a month, which office he held till 1863. He made daily visits to the prison, covering the distance from Fairfax to the point on his fiery steed almost as quickly as an automobile could negotiate the journey. He was really an accomplished surgeon and physician, as he amply proved during a large practice in later years.

He was my warm friend, as he was of everyone honored with his acquaintance. From him I learned much concerning the very early history of the State Prison. From him I learned what does not appear elsewhere, that in those early days severe punishments were rare. Estell was deeply opposed to the whipping post, and floggings were only administered in exceptional cases of insurrection. He regarded Estell as a good-natured fellow, endeavoring to live up to his lights, but easily imposed upon and therefore led into many errors.

The evidence of Dr. Taliaferro before the Assembly Investigating Committee follows:

Dr. Alfred Taliaferro, being duly sworn before the State Prison Committee March 10, 1855, says:

I reside within five miles of the State Prison; have been employed by General Estell as visiting physician at the prison for the last eighteen months; I am there often; when it is necessary I am there every day; the management of the prison has been rather loose, but the liberties given to convicts have generally been to those that had but a short term to serve; they usually had a great number of trustees; some ten or fifteen trustees; trustees were sent after me when anyone was sick; about thrity guards usually employed about the prison; have seen some intemperance or rowdyism among the guards, usually in the evening, but the guards, having formerly been of the class called rangers, are very brave and desperate men, but somewhat addicted to dissipation; I believe that much of this intemperance is not known to General Estell, and have frequently known guards to be negligent, and by that negligence to allow the escape of prisoners, but in such cases they concealed their negligence from the captain of the guard by telling some plausible story;

I have known diseases among convicts from the use of bad flour; some one or two that I attended to and eight or ten others that I heard of, such as colic, cramps, and spasms, and in such cases I have given immediate notice of the fact to the superintendent to have it corrected; it has usually been corrected; I am employed by the month and not by the visit; only one died by disease since I have been in attendance, and one other died suddenly in his bed without any premonitory symptoms; I do not think the prisoners are safe in private hands, nor that it can ever be made so; I am opposed to the practice of farming out the convicts; it is not a correct system; I have known convicts working on Watson's place and also on Thompson's place; these were preemption claims on what is called Bucklew's ranch;

I sent for eight convicts the year before last to get out my potatoes; they worked three or four days; they had two guards with them from the prison and some of the time more; they stayed at my house overnight; they slept upstairs; they were not chained or locked, but the guard slept below; the house was not locked; there were none escaped while at my house; afterward they dug potatoes at Phoenix Ranch, about four miles from the prison; they stayed there over night; they formed a plan to escape from my house (as one of the prisoners has since told me), and the only thing that prevented them was the dogs; they were afraid of the dogs or were apprehensive they would bark and rally the guards and others.

Liquor To Blame

The foregoing testimony is a fair synopsis of the mass of evidence accumulated by the Assembly Investigating Committee. One thing noticeable is the absence of any reference to the open gambling which prevailed to such a shocking extent in later years. Owing to the absence of walls, a dealer might hesitate to open a game for fear that some enterprising convict might escape, taking with him layout, bank roll, and all.

The really serious charges of mismanagement against the prison administration rested wholly on the free use of liquor by officers and prisoners alike, the intimate relations between the female convicts and their legal guardians, and the abuse of the trusty system. These conditions the committee admitted were not entirely commendable. They are barely touched on in the Committee's report—just enough to indicate that they were deemed unworthy of serious concern, nothing for anyone to kick about. Further inquiry shows that while some legislative Pharisees believed that the practice of selling liquor to prisoners was questionable, the majority impression was the other way. Why, they asked, should these unfortunates, deprived of their liberty, be also deprived of the staff of life?

The sole and only question appealing to the legislative committee was that of walling the convicts in and securing them in escape-proof cells.

By a mathematical calculation, not unlike the rosy prospective profits that the tenderfoot figures out when embarking in a chicken ranch enterprise, the committee estimated that the State could make money by dumping Estell and taking over the whole institution, and constructing the wall and necessary buildings on the public's own account.

Hard Bargainer

Estell greatly preferred to continue his lease, provided the State lived up to its part of the contract in the matter of construction. But the committee would not hear of it. Then Estell was willing to retire on the basis of his losses, to wit: $127,000. The following correspondence shows the State to have been a hard bargainer:

Estell's Offer To Sell

> To Col. Whiting, Chairman State Prison Committee:
>
> I propose to take $127,000 for the State Prison contract, payable in seven percent bonds. If, however, the payment should be made in eight percent bonds, I am willing to allow the State their difference in value.

I will take the original cost of the steam engines and brick machinery, and the estimated value of the other property, payable in stone and bricks at their market value. The valuation to be made by three Commissioners—one to be named by the State, one by myself and the two to name a third.

—J. M. Estell, Lessee State Prison,
Sacramento City, March 16, 1855.

The State's Reply

Resolved, that John T. Crenshaw, a member of this Committee, be authorized to state to James M. Estell:

First. That the Committee on behalf of the State cannot give any encouragement that the State will accept his proposition, dated March 16, 1855, made by him.

Second. That the Committee will recommend to the two branches of the Legislature to purchase the State Prison contract and pay therefore one hundred thousand dollars in State bonds, payable in ten years from the date of their issue, with semi-annual interest at the rate of seven percent per annum.

Also, that the State purchase the sixteen acres of land belonging to the brickyard, the engine, brick machinery, and other valuable improvements at their appraised value, to be appraised by three Commissioners, one Commissioner to be appointed by General Estell, and the other two to be elected by a joint convention of the two branches of the Legislature. All this property [is] to be paid for by the State in brick and stone manufactured or worked by the convicts, to be delivered at San Francisco at market prices. B. C. Whiting, Chairman.

Estell's Acceptance

Sacramento City, March 18th, 1855.
Chairman Committee on State Prison

Sir:

In answer to your communication of yesterday, will say I could, by a sale to other parties, or by hiring out the prisoners to contractors, make a much larger amount of money than by the acceptance of the terms proposed by the Committee; but I am fully persuaded the convicts cannot be kept safely with the present means for their confinement.

If the Committee would recommend an appropriation to build the prison and prison walls, I would greatly prefer holding the present contract; but, having been assured by yourself there is no possibility of such a recommendation, and fearing from the exposed condition of the prison a successful revolution might occur while I am responsible, I am compelled, reluctantly, to accept the terms proposed, to be recommended by the Committee in Mr. Whiting's resolution.

I am, very respectfully yours,

—J. M. Estell, Lessee State Prison

10.

LEGISLATURE CREATES A BOARD OF PRISON DIRECTORS TO TAKE POSSESSION OF SAN QUENTIN WITHOUT PROVIDING FOR PAYING THE LESSEE SUM AGREED UPON AS A COMPROMISE OR CLAIM

The Legislature of 1855 did not accept the offer of Estell to sell his lease for $100,000, a sum materially less than his losses had been, as told in the preceding chapter. Instead, confusion was confounded by the passage of an act passed May 7, 1855, creating a Board of Prison Directors of three members. Governor Bigler apparently was not trusted to name these officers. They were chosen at a joint session of both houses. The names of these directors-elect were: Richard N. Snowden, William H. Palmer, and J. L. Love.

Snowden was already a prison inspector. He was related to Lord Charles S. Fairfax, either a nephew or first cousin. Like his lordship, he was a very handsome man, rather erratic, but courteous and companionable. In later years he came to a sad end. Like most of his generation he had a taste for liquor that led him into prolonged sprees, followed by protracted sessions with remorse, and periods of total abstinence. After one of these unequal contests with King Alcohol, he announced to numerous friends that if he ever got drunk again he would kill himself. He was as good as his word. Another debauch came, and as soon as he sobered up he went into the rear of a livery stable in San Rafael and shot himself in the head, dying instantly. John L. Love was a lawyer-politician, who cut some figure in both activities, and became, long after, Attorney-General of the State. W. H. Palmer I can only locate as a San Francisco business man, more or less versed in politics.

FULL POWERS GIVEN

The salary of the prison directors was fixed at $3,500 a year each, with free quarters at San Quentin Prison, where they were required to reside. They were given the most plenary powers. They were to take possession of San Quentin Prison on June 1, 1858, were directed to name a warden at an unnamed salary, and a deputy warden at $1,800 a year and a chaplain at $1,200 a year, and other officers they deemed fit. They were authorized to purchase supplies, either in open market or by contract, according to their best judgment. They were instructed to build immediately a substantial wall around the prison and necessary prison buildings, and also to make rules and regulations concerning the discipline and the nature of their labor.

The Attorney-General of the State had advised the Legislature that the act of 1851 was not terminable at pleasure, that the contract with Estell could only be annulled by the courts upon showing breaches of the same by the lessee. Yet any layman can see at a glance that the entire act was in gross violation of the lessee's rights. It practically stripped him of all his equities except the serious responsibility under his bond.

The old prison inspectors were not retired. Under the ruling of the Attorney-General, they could not be. Hitherto they had served entirely without salary or even an expense account, barring only the sum of five dollars paid to each as expenses while traveling around in search for a suitable site for the prison. By an act of 1855, in a burst of generosity, they were not only given salaries of $1,200, but, in addition thereto, four years of back salary at the same rate. By this retroactive procedure each Inspector received a gift of $5,000, which was probably acceptable.

STATE OF CORNER

By the Act, the official salaries were made payable monthly out of any money not otherwise appropriated in the

State Treasury. But nothing whatever was said about the cost of maintenance—the payment for food, clothing, drugs, and various supplies. Probably the solons expected that these items would be cared for by the various outputs of prison labor.

By this brilliantly executed maneuver, Estell worked the State into a corner. He had secured a complete release from an agreement that probably meant ruin. And at the same time the financial affairs had become so profoundly muddled that the lessee had absolutely equitable claims for a huge amount against the State, which no honest legislature could ignore. In the end, he doubtless had a conviction that the solons would turn to him again with a far different proposition than the contract of 1851.

He had good grounds for this belief. Never before was a public institution so hopelessly entangled. Three distinct bodies claimed jurisdiction over it—the original prison inspectors, the Board of Prison Commissioners, composed of the Lieutenant-Governor, the Controller, and Secretary of State, and the newly created State Prison Directors. These more or less antagonistic bodies were certain to get into a squabble, and like the gentleman in the opera who was confronted at an unusual hour by his wedded wife and mother-in-law, the time was opportune for the lessee to take a header and disappear beneath the water until the clouds cleared on the political horizon.

Estell's Agreement

Herewith is a copy of the agreement by which Estell turned over San Quentin Prison to the State Prison directors:

> Whereas, by virtue of an act of the legislature of the State of California, passed April 25, A.D. 1851, the said State entered into a contract with James M. Estell, whereby the said Estell was and is bound to receive and safely keep the State convicts for the period of ten years from the date of said

contract, and in consideration thereof was and is entitled to the labor of said convicts for ten years. And, whereas, it is believed that the interests of the State and the execution of the laws would be best served by a relinquishment on the part of said lessee of the convicts now in his charge and the remaining portion of the unexpired contract from and after the date hereof;

Now, therefore, be it known, that the said James M. Estell as lessee of the State prison and R. N. Snowden, J. L. Love, and Wm. H. Palmer, directors appointed under and by virtue of a law passed May 7, 1855, have this day entered into and executed the following agreement, *viz.*:

The said James M. Estell agrees and hereby relinquishes to the said directors, acting on the part of the State of California, the State convicts, buildings, lands, and appurtenances thereunto belonging, and the property of the State, together with the unexpired portion of his contract and all right to the labor and service of said convicts from and after the date of these presents, in compliance with the provision of the act of May 7, 1855, all control over the convicts, grounds, and buildings; and furthermore agrees and stipulates, that he will in no manner interfere with the directors in the assumption of the contract and the full control of the convicts, or in the performance of their duties under the act of May 7, 1855, from and after the signing and ensealing hereof, and that he will not hereafter seek to disturb the State in the custody of the convicts and prison grounds and buildings, obtained by said lessee under the act of April 25, 1851.

And it is furthermore agreed and understood that, in relinquishing the unexpired portion of the contract and the convicts, as above mentioned, the said lessee relinquishes no legal or equitable claim he may have, or claim to have against the State for damages or relief in consequence of alleged failure or neglect on the part of the State to perform or fulfill the provisions of the contract of 1851, prior to the first day of June, 1855, or for any damages to which he may be justly entitled for injuries sustained or claimed to have been sustained in consequences of the act of May 7, 1855; provided, however, that, as the said directors have no authority other than to take possession of said convicts, prison grounds, and prison, under the law, and disclaim all right or intention to take into consideration, or interfere in any manner with, the claims of the said lessee against the State, it is distinctly understood that nothing in this agreement shall be so construed to admit, recognize, deny, or prejudice the validity of any such claim or claims.

Act Was Void

The whole act was void on its face, had Estell chosen to fight it in the courts. But here the General showed talents of a Napoleonic order. Possibly he had come to the end of his rope financially, and was only too willing to go into a temporary eclipse. Anyhow, he quit. He turned over to the new board of Prison Directors the entire property, real and personal, steam brickyard, the sixteen acres with the queer title, three large schooners, tools and general equipment, several million bricks, and many thousand cubic feet of dressed rock, as appeared by a lengthy schedule.

11.

WHILE THE FINANCES OF THE STATE WERE AT A LOW EBB PRISONERS WERE NOT PROPERLY CLOTHED OR FED, AND A NEW BOARD OF DIRECTORS APPEALED TO LEGISLATURE FOR HELP

With such a condition as described in the preceding chapter, the State Prison Directors took possession of San Quentin on June 1, 1855. The trusty system was practically abolished, the guard force largely increased and promptly paid, which had not been the case in the last six months during the Estell regime, who left behind him a long arrearage of debts due to his faithful men, all of which were subsequently liquidated. But one good and immediate result of the change was that the number of escapes was reduced to the extent of seventy-five percent.

But with divided authority, almost of necessity a conflict of opinion followed. The prison directors got at loggerheads with the Board of Prison Commissioners. The prison inspectors disagreed with both, and the directors themselves fell out. Worst of all, Governor Bigler was hostile, largely because the State Prison directors had been appointed over his head. He had written a private letter to Estell, advising him by innuendo to hold the fort against their pretensions. Under these depressing conditions, the directors took charge of San Quentin Prison. According to their legislative instructions, they proceeded to let a contract for a wall 500 feet on each side, enclosing approximately six acres of land.

Contract For Wall

The contract was let to James Smiley. The specifications are exceedingly obscure. The wall was to be twenty feet high, the first ten feet to be of rough hewn stone set in cement, the second ten feet of brick set in mortar. The width at the base was four feet wide, tapering to two feet at the top, surmounted by a stone cap four feet wide. The entire structure was to rest on a rubble foundation of an unmentioned depth. The brick and stone and convict labor were to be furnished by the State. The contractor furnished only the lime, cement, sand, and a few free expert masons and bricklayers.

By the terms of the contract the State was to pay forty cents a cubic foot of stone in place, and $15 a thousand for brick in place, and iron work for gates at ten cents per pound. As the State furnished the brick, stone, and convict labor free, the figures were scandalous. As a matter of fact, it was not fully completed by the above-mentioned date. Some idea of the cost can be gathered from the fact that warrants had been drawn in the contractor's favor for $125,000 and registered for payment with the State Treasurer. At that time the credit of the State was at a very low ebb. Its debts were payable about a year after they were due. Valid and approved claims were registered with the Treasurer, after which they bore interest at the rate of seven percent per annum.

Meanwhile, the financial condition of the institution continued to go from bad to worse. The rosy anticipation that sales of rock and brick would suffice to feed and clothe the convicts was not realized to an appreciable extent. San Francisco was in the throes of its first big slump. The "diggings" showed plain traces of giving out. Prophets of evil, who have ever been plentiful on the peninsula, furnished mathematical data to prove that the city would soon be uninhabited, and the whole region around the bay return to primitive barbarism. While the population was suffering from this acute attack of doldrums, the city was a poor place to market stone and brick. Therefore, the State Prison Directors were compelled to purchase their supplies on credit of the State, for which no legislative provisions had been made. Under these depressing circumstances such necessary articles as food and clothing were not obtainable from the larger and more cautious firms, and could be bought only from a few speculators, willing to take a gambler's chance, with profits ranging from 100 percent or more above normal. It might be noted here that the State Controller's warrants were received by banks at a discount of twenty-five percent.

That the affairs of the prison were involved in a frightful mess goes without saying. The wall contract created a scandal, and was bitterly denounced by opposing politicians and the press. The general management of the prison, under Love, Palmer, and Snowden, was characterized as a retrograde movement, while Estell was eulogized as an enlightened philanthropist.

What became of this board of prison directors is one of the dark mysteries of the State—that is, what became of them officially. Personally, they did not die. I knew two of them, Dick Snowden and John Lord Love, years after they disappeared from the official list in a most uncanny way. On May 5, 1855, they had been appointed for terms ranging from one to three years, the terms of each to be determined by lot. It seems unlikely that they would throw up comfortable jobs with salaries of $3,500 a year. Neither did the Governor have any power to remove undesirable incumbents from office, either by the old Constitution or by legislative enactment. The most careful search at Sacramento and in files of contemporary papers fail to indicate how that vacancies came about, but on January 1, 1856, Governor Bigler appointed an entirely new board, with additional handles to their official names, namely: E. S. McKenzie, State Prison director and warden; Alexander Bell, State Prison director and secretary, and E. Wilson, director and president of the board. The modest "E" in Mr. Wilson's name stood for "Ezekiel." He became a famous railroad lobbyist and dealer in men in later days. The firm of Wilson and Broughton was the first of famous freebooter concerns that gripped California for nearly fifty years. Mr. Broughton's first name was Napoleon. Not to know Zeke Wilson and "Nap" Broughton was to argue yourself unknown in the old days.

Financial Collapse

They took possession of the institution the next day, apparently without any resistance from the old board. On January 19 the new board presented a memorial that indicates clearly the profound financial collapse which had overtaken the institution.

To the Honorable, the Senate and Assembly of the State of California:

It is with unfeigned regret that the undersigned State Prison directors are compelled so soon after being installed in office, to call upon the Legislature for pecuniary aid, in order to enable us to execute the duties imposed upon us by the law under which we are acting.

A brief statement of the condition in which we found the prison and its inmates upon assuming the duties of our office will be necessary to a full and proper understanding of our present position:

At the time we took charge of the prison, not more than three days' supplies were on hand, rendering an immediate outlay of money or exercise of credit absolutely indispensable to meet the needs of the prisoners.

The credit of the prison is such as to render it impossible to obtain necessary supplies without submitting to executions which would be ruinous to the interests of the State, and render the support of the prison onerous in the extreme.

The Directors present the institution to you without means or credit, and having in charge and looking to the directors for food and clothing, more than four hundred and eighty persons, inlcuding officers, guards, employees, and convicts.

Common decency and humanity require that some provision be made by the State for the proper care of those that have been condemned for the violation of her laws. The directors do not deem it reputable or humane for a State to punish felons by starvation, or by withholding such articles of clothing as will, at least, hide nakedness, and form some protection against the inclemencies of the season.

The board of directors would further represent:

That the occupation of the convicts has theretofore mainly been making brick, quarrying, and cutting stone for San Francisco and other markets. The former business it is impossible to pursue during the rainy season, and the demand for stone during the same season is so slight that the directors cannot, with any certainty, calculate upon deriving any revenue from the sale of brick or stone within the ensuing five months.

The convicts at present are employed in grading the prison grounds and in digging clay for making brick, to be used as soon as the season will allow. So deeply are we impressed with the necessity of legislative aid to relieve us from our present embarrassments that we feel authorized to briefly recapitulate our situation and urge, in the most respectful manner, the earliest action of the Legislature upon the subject of this memorial.

We are destitute of supplies with which to meet the daily demands of the prison.

A large portion of the convicts are in immediate want of the most common and ordinary articles of clothing.

The prison has no credit, or only such credit as will enable the directors to obtain supplies at double the market prices.

At present we cannot employ convict labor so as to make it if any value toward the support of the prison.

Lack of acquaintance with the cost of supporting the prison renders it impossible for the directors to fix the amount of money that should be appropriated to relieve our present and future necessities, but the directors will state from the best information they can gain, that the expenses for this year will not fall short of fifteen thousand dollars per month; we shall not, therefore, ask for any specific amount as an appropriation, but submit the same to the discretion of your honorable bodies.

The directors would further represent:

That at the present time there is one hundred and fifty convicts lodged in one room, so that the erection of a new prison is absolutely necessary. ALEX BELL, E. S. McKENZIE, E. WILSON, State Prison Directors.

I sign the above report, because I agree with my colleagues that not less than the sum mentioned above will be sufficient to pay the expenses of the prison, but state also, that upon a careful calculation of the figures, if the prison is more properly managed, will amount to at least 50 percent more than the estimate set down as above, and further, if nothing is done previous to the first of February next, the prisoners will be destitute, and the directors forced to throw them upon the charity of your honorable body.

ALEX BELL, State Prison Director

Note: Since the above was in type I have found that there was no mystery at all about the succession of the Prison directors. By the original act, the board was made elective, the appointed board holding office only until January 1, 1856. At the State election of November, 1855, Messrs. McKenzie, Wilson, and Bell were elected and took charge on

January 1, 1856. I was misled by reading a synopsis of the act, not the act itself. J.H.W.

12.

THE STATE'S FIRST EXPERIMENT IN MANAGING A PRISON A COSTLY AFFAIR, ESPECIALLY THE BUILDING OF THE WALL, WHICH WAS SCORED BY A LEGISLATIVE INVESTIGATING COMMITTEE

I had quite omitted to mention in the last chapter that Director W. H. Palmer made a highly sensational disappearance from the official viewpoint. Whether he died, resigned, or became a fugitive from justice, the record showeth not. All we know with certainty is that on October 17, 1855, Governor Bigler appointed John Madden to succeed W. H. Palmer as State Prison Director, without deigning to state how the vacancy had occurred. The Directors had formerly classified themselves according to the duties each saw fit to perform, thus: R. N. Snowden, President; J. L. Love, Warden; W. H. Palmer, Secretary. It was therefore Madden's job to succeed Palmer as Secretary, but according to the evidence he was never able to secure the books. He went out of office with his confreres on January 1, 1856.

The appeal of the new Directors for ready cash to purchase food to feed the starving prisoners at San Quentin found a prompt response. Inside of a week an emergency bill was rushed through both houses of the legislature, appropriating the sum of $15,000 to be expended solely for provisions. This relieved temporarily the immediate danger of starvation.

In the meantime there must have been a howl of indignation against the antics of the old Board. This may be judged from the fact that two of the members presented a memorial to the legislature requesting an investigation, in the following words:

To the Senate and Assembly of the State of California: The undersigned, composing the late Board of State Prison Directors, beg leave respectfully to represent that, as gross misrepresentations have been published in relation to their official acts, they desire the appointment of the select committee, with full power to scrutinize every transaction sanctioned by the Board or Warden.

The books, vouchers, and contracts exhibit the names of all persons who have transacted business for or with the Board, and we hope you will authorize and empower the committee to compel such persons to appear before them and testify, and that you will further authorize and empower said committee to visit the prison, examine the wall, as well as remeasure and estimate the work.

In conclusion we beg leave to add that we have a report nearly completed and which will be transmitted in a few days, or if you so instruct, will be delivered to the committee, as well as copies of all contracts, books, and vouchers.

—R. N. Snowden
John L. Love
Sacramento, January 24, 1856

An investigation followed, not so much because Messrs. Snowden and Love desired it, as because the circumstances demanded it. Probably the most remarkable state of affairs was uncovered that ever came to the attention of the people of this free republic.

It would require several pages of this work to cover the evidence accumulated by the joint committee of Senate and Assembly appointed to investigate the affairs of San Quentin Prison. The best I can do is to present a summary that will furnish a general idea of how the institution was run during the first attempt at direct control by the State.

In the first place it appeared conclusively that the Directors never acted as a whole or collectively, but as if each had complete and absolute control of the institution. Love made a contract for the construction of the prison wall with James Smiley, involving, as it afterwards appeared, the sum of $180,000. He admitted that he had not consulted any of his colleagues concerning the contract further than that Snowden had told him to make any arrangement relative to the wall that seemed "equitable and right." Love further stated that he had let the contract to Smiley, whom he had met in a casual way, without advertising or seeking proposals from anyone else. He was not familiar with the cost of materials or construction, but mentioned the little incident of letting the contract to Directors Snowden and Palmer, who had yawned and said in an absent-minded way that they opined it was OK. All three Directors had made individual contracts and ordered great quantities of supplies purely on their own motion. What seems strangest still was that the Directors individually drew orders on the State Controller for huge sums of money, without any particulars whatever, and these singular drafts were honored by the Controller just the same as if they had been regularly audited and approved claims, passed on, and approved by the Board of Prison Directors in their collective capacity.

Orders had been given by Love and controller's warrants drawn in favor of Contractor Smiley for $125,000, and a large balance remained. The basis of the claims were measurements for rock work and work in place, made by Love, but when the same were re-measured by the committee's engineer, there was no such yardage there. The difference between the figures of Love and the engineer, when reduced to dollars and cents, amounted to the tidy sum of $39,978—against the State, of course.

Moreover, various contractors and builders testified that the wall could have been built for the sum of $50,000 with a good margin of profit, instead of $180,000 as charged. On this point the committee reported, and the legislature concurred, that $61,000 was ample compensation. As already Controller's warrants had been issued and registered by the Treasurer, the legislature passed a bill hurriedly, directing him to cancel and annul the registry of these warrants and refuse payment if presented. Lest the Treasurer forget, any lapse on his part was declared a felony and made punishable by a fine of $50,000 and confinement in the State prison for two years. This enactment, however, was declared void by the courts as against innocent holders of this particular "State Scrip," and as it was all found to have passed into innocent hands, the warrants in due season were presented and paid. However, Smiley was never paid the large balance claimed to be due him.

With further regard to the wall, it had not been built in the form of a 500-foot square as required in the Act creating the Board of Prison Directors. On the contrary, the south side had been made 593 feet long without visible cause, entirely destroying the symmetrical appearance of the whole structure.

Director John Madden, who succeeded Director Palmer on October 17th, testified that he had never seen the contract for the construction of the wall till December 5th, when he found it in the Controller's office; that Director Snowden had previously stated to him that he had never seen or signed the contract, but when Mr. Madden had seen it as above stated, the names of Snowden and Palmer were attached as signatures. He had made many demands for the prison books but never was able even to get a look at them. In this connection Director Love and Clerk Brady testified that the books had been so carelessly kept and were otherwise such masses of errors and inaccuracies that they were valueless for the purpose of investigation. The Director thereupon presented a "synopsis" of the books, which he averred was ample for any reasonable purpose. And that was as near as the committee ever came to seeing them.

The startling sum total of it all was that in the space of seven months in this primitive attempt at public ownership the Directors had involved the State to the extent of $388,000. More than half of this went to the wall account and to the purchase of Estell's private personal property, by which he realized enough to pay his debts and get into good standing again. But even at that it seemed clear enough that the future cost of maintaining a prison, officered and maintained by the State, could not be less than $300,000. In the terribly embarrassing financial condition of the state, this was unthinkably calamitous.

The investigating committee gave a fine old blast to the old Board for extravagance, for riding roughshod over every limitation of law and common sense, referring to their affairs and turning the entire matter over to the Attorney-General for appropriate action. Clearly the solons were harking back to the good old times of J. M. Estell, when the maintenance of the prison cost the people nothing at all.

13.

STATE MANAGEMENT OF SAN QUENTIN PRISON PROVED SO DISASTROUS THAT THE LEGISLATURE, ON THE REPORT OF A COMMITTEE, AGAIN AUTHORIZED A LEASE WHICH WAS GIVEN TO ESTELL

What seemed the most disheartening feature of the situation was the statement of the new Board of Prison Directors that they could not do much better than their predecessors. Directors McKenzie and Wilson thought the prison might worry through with an appropriation of $250,000, together with an appropriation of $95,000 for indispensable new buildings. Director Bell, on the other hand, presented tabulated statements showing that a minimum appropriation for the support of the institution could not be less than $329,000, together with a building appropriation of $100,000.

As this latter estimate amounted approximately to one-third of the entire revenue of the State at that period of its existence, it was simply out of the question. The State was crushed under a load of high interest bearing debt and official extravagance. The Legislature of 1850, in order to raise immediate revenue, had authorized a large bond issue at the then current rate of three percent a month, or thirty-six percent a year. Other bond issues bearing a very high interest rate had followed. Nearly all but the three-percent-a-month bonds had been retired by 1856, but the credit of the State had suffered to the extent that it was a year behind in the payment of its legal debts. Clearly the State was unable to finance the prison on its own resources, according to the estimates of its own officers. The concluding paragraphs in the report of the joint investigating committee indicated that a radical change was imperative.

From the Committee Report:

> From the above statement it appears that the contractor for the wall has been overpaid in the sum of $65,200, and from the books of the Directors it appears also that the contractor still holds certified accounts to the amount of $80,000, which accounts have not been audited; $32,000 of this amount is for supplies alleged to have been furnished to the prison, and $48,000 certified to by the Directors for the purpose of indemnifying the contractor against the loss by the depreciation of a State scrip. The total amount outstanding against the State, as shown by the books of the Directors and the report of the Controller, is $128,244,66. The Directors, it appears, voluntarily and without the color of authority certified to this $48,000, or thirty percent, in addition to the amount certified in the contract. Your committee is clearly of the opinion that this amount was not wholly unauthorized.
>
> Your committee was unable to obtain the original books of the prison which were withheld from the committee for reasons unknown, except for the reason as stated by

Major Love, that there was so much error and irregularity in the manner of keeping them that he deemed it essential to have a correct copy made, which copies were the only books presented to your committee. Mr. Brady, who was employed for some time as Clerk, states the same thing.

The report made by the present Board of Directors shows the expenses of the State Prison for the month of January to be $23,243,52. At this rate it will require an appropriation of $270,000 annually to support the prison and defray its expenses. The Board, however, widely differ on this point, as Mr. Bell, one of the present Directors, estimates the cost of the prison for the ensuing year at $329,700. In addition to the foregoing amount, there will have to be an expenditure of at least $100,000 for the erection of buildings necessary to contain the prisoners.

The lease between James M. Estell and the State of Marin Island expires on the first day of June, 1856, and unless there be some provision made by the State, there will be no place to confine the prisoners at present employed therein, amounting to about one hundred. The present building at San Quentin is already filled to utmost capacity, there being now four convicts in each cell, and about one hundred and fifty thrown together in one room.

From all the facts, as set forth in the above report, it would seem that the most advisable course for the State to pursue is again to revert to the contract or leasing system upon the most reasonable terms and to the most responsible person or persons. The State will thus know how much will be required for the actual support and maintenance of the State Prison, and then her expenditures will cease.

The report of the investigating committee was presented to the Legislature on February 21, 1856. It must have struck a responsive chord among the membership of both houses, for on March 21, 1856, a bill was passed enlarging the powers of the old Board of Prison Commissioners:

1. The Lieutenant-Governor, Controller, and Treasurer are hereby constituted a Board of Commissioners, whose duty it shall be to lease the State Prison grounds and property, together with convict labor of this State, for a period of five years; at a price not to exceed fifteen thousand dollars per month, and in conformity with the provisions of the act.

2. In any contract entered into by said Board, provision shall be made for the erection of such buildings and for making the improvements on the property owned or leased by the State, at the expense of the lessee, for such purposes as will conduce to the safety and convenience of keeping, working, clothing, feeding, and providing medicine and medical attendance for the convicts of the State, and without subjecting the State in any way to any payment of any amount whatever for the same. Such work to be done in accordance with a plan to be approved by the Board of Commissioners, and at such time and place and of such material as they may order.

3. The Board of Commissioners shall make such rules and regulations governing said prison, alter and amend same at pleasure, and cause them to be observed by the infliction of such penalties as they may deem proper.

6. The Board of Commissioners shall require the lessee to execute bonds in the penal sum of not less than

$200,000, with two or more good and sufficient sureties to be approved by said Board for the faithful performance of his contract.

8. An act entitled "An Act for Securing the State Prison Convicts," passed April 25th, one thousand eight hundred and fifty-one, and so much of section first of an Act, entitled "An Act for the Government of the State Prison," passed May Seventh, one thousand eight hundred and fifty-five, as relates to the future election of State Prison Directors, and so much of the other sections of said Act as conflicts with the provisions of this Act, are hereby repealed.

Aside from granting powers to make a new lease and legislate concerning the immediate conduct of the Prison, this act changed the situation in a radical way. For one thing it cleared up forever the old Act of 1851, thereby getting rid of such dead timber, among which might be mentioned the State Prison Directors. The new State Prison Directors were practically legislated out of office by the action providing that no further elections should be held for Directors. In fact, as will be seen later, by a gentlemen's agreement the three Directors agreed to surrender their authority and fade away provided they were paid one year's salary.

It did not take the Board of State Prison Commissioners long to conclude arrangements. More than likely, the arrangements were cut and dried before the Act enlarging the powers of the State Prison Commissioners had fairly passed. This may be judged from the following preamble of a report:

> Hon. J. T. Farley, Speaker of House of Assembly:
>
> The undersigned Commissioners appointed by Act creating a Board of State Prison Commissioners and defining their duties, approved March 21, 1856, beg leave to submit the following report:

That on the 26th day of March, 1856, they leased the State Prison grounds with all the property attached thereto, as also the labor of the State Prison convicts, to James M. Estell, for the period of five years from the 26th day of March, 1856, and that they have made formal delivery of the same to the said lessee, for the particulars of which we refer you to a copy of the lease and Schedule "A" herein accompanying, and also a copy of a "supplemental agreement," all of which is respectfully submitted.

If it is the intention of the Legislature to establish a branch of the State Prison at some other point than the one now occupied, we would suggest that an appropriation be made to enable the commissioners, or whoever else may be designated to perform the duty, to procure a site for the erection of the aforementioned prison, and also to obtain the drawings of the necessary plans to be used in the construction of the prison buildings.

We would also state that to conduct the proper construction of the buildings and walls, contracted to be erected for the State by the lessee, it will require frequent visits of one or all of the commissioners during the progress of the work, involving an expense much greater than is provided for in the act creating the Board of State Prison Commissioners. We would, therefore, suggest that an appropriation equal to the actual expenses necessary to be incurred be made for that purpose.

After a careful personal examination of the premises your commissioners are saitsfied that the attention of the present Board of State Prison Directors is not required at the State Prison as now conducted, and would therefore recommend that their salaries be ordered paid for one year and the office abolished. A great public necessity requires this course, and we have no doubt but that the incumbents will yield a cheerful and hearty concurrence in the above suggestion.

In making the foregoing remarks and suggestions we may have departed from a strict line of duty, but we indulge the hope that they will be received by your honorable body, and all whom they may concern in the sprit in which they are intended. Respectfully your ob't servants,

—R. M. Anderson
G. W. Whitman
Henry Bates
Board of State Prison Commissioners

The new lease to Estell, as will be seen, was one of those unusual arrangements that became profitable to both sides of the bargain.

14.

GENERAL ESTELL AGAIN GETS INTO FINANCIAL DIFFICULTIES UNDER HIS NEW LEASE BECAUSE THE STATE FAILED TO LIVE UP TO ITS AGREEMENT TO PAY HIM $10,000 A MONTH

The lease made by the Board of State Prison Commissioners with J. M. Estell referred to in the preceding chapter is too lengthy a document to be more than mentioned here.

It described all the property, real and personal, leased by the State to James M. Estell, until the end of a full term of five years. The State of California agreed to pay to J. M. Estell the full and just sum of $10,000 on the last day of each calendar month on notification to do so by the lessee.

The lessee, in consideration of the use and occupation of said premises and the labor of the State Prison convicts and the monthly payments aforesaid, agreed to receive and take charge of all convicts confined or to be confined, and to keep them safely at his own proper expense, and that he further provide under the direction of the Board of State Prison Commissioners, necessary guards and officers and "furnish to said State Prison convicts, suitable and wholesome food and drink and medical attendance and sufficient clothing and to treat such convicts humanely and with all degree of kindness consistent with their security and safety."

The lessee further agreed that he would, at his own cost and expense, erect such buildings and walls as directed by the State Board of Prison Commissioners, according to plans and specifications prepared by them, "without subjecting the State to any manner of expense for the same."

By the said agreement or lease, Estell waived all claims, whether legal or equitable, against the State arising out of his former connection with the State. This is a blanket clause, though some of the leading claims so waived are enumerated. These waivers aggregated a huge sum and really represented the price paid for the lease.

The lessee agreed to return the property to the State at the expiration of five years from March 25, 1856, in as good condition as reasonable wear and tear would permit. The lessee was required to give a bond of $200,000 for the faithful performance of the terms of the lease.

But by far the most important part of the lease was a supplementary agreement by which the system of farming out the labor of convicts to subcontractors engaged in manufacturing pursuits was first introduced into the prison administration of California. It endured for more than thirty years, and constituted during that period an impassable barrier against any measure of prison reform.

> Memorandum of an agreement made and entered into between R. M. Anderson, Lieutenant-Governor of the State of California, G. W. Whitman, Controller of the State of California, and Henry Bates, treasurer of the State of California, creating a Board of Prison Commissioners and defining their duties, approved March 21, 1856. Party of the First Part; and James M. Estell, of the County of San Francisco, State of California, Party of the Second Part; WITNESSETH:
>
> That whereas, the said party of the first part, did, on the 26th day of March, A.D. 1856, lease to the said party of the second part the State Prison grounds at Point San Quentin in the County of Marin, and State of California, together with all the property attached thereto, and the labor of the State Prison convicts, for the term of five years from the 26th day of March, 1856;
>
> Now therefore, in explanation of said contract, and to confirm to the said party of the second part the full benefit of the same, it is hereby agreed by the said party of the first part that the said party of the second part shall have the privilege and be at full liberty to

work the State Prison convicts at any and all mechanical branches of business that he may choose, provided that the said convicts shall not be employed at any kind or description of labor that shall greatly endanger their lives, health, limbs, or safekeeping. It is further agreed and understood between the said party of the first part and the said party of the second part that nothing herein contained shall effect, in any manner, the sureties of the said party of the second part, or their liability on the bond given by him at the time of executing the contract referred to herein.

In witness whereof the said R. M. Anderson, G. W. Whitman, and Henry Bates, constituting the Board of State Prison Commissioners, party of the first part, and James M. Estell, party of the second part, have hereunto set their hands and seals this third day of April A.D. one thousand eight hundred and fifty six.

(Seal) R. M. Anderson
(Seal) G. W. Whitman
(Seal) Henry Bates
Board of Commissioners
(Seal) James M. Estell

A long list of personal property concerned is appended to the lease.

Upon the resumption of his lease Estell showed evidence of much executive ability. Under the State Prison Directors the official list included sixty-four employees, some of them with fancy salaries, to guard a little over four hundred prisoners. He pared the list down to thirty-nine. Under the direction of the Board of Prison Commissioners he constructed a new cell building, a large workshop (which burned down in 1875), officers' quarters, and the old office building where the later Boards of Prison Directors have met down to the present day. He kept a close and accurate cost of building expenses, and it was proved and admitted that he spent over $77,000 on this account alone. He made a very favorable contract with Daniel Green and A. B. Melvill to employ prison labor in manufacturing, paying therefore fifty cents a day for the first three months, seventy-five cents a day for the second three months, and one dollar a day for the remainder of the lease. Estell was on the high road of making good his losses when the State again flagrantly defaulted in its undertaking to pay the lessee $10,000 a month in cash. The story is best told in Estell's own words embodied in the following communication to the Legislature:

> To the Senate and the Assembly of the State of California:
>
> Gentlemen: It becomes my duty as lessee of the State Prison of this State, to make known to you the condition of that institution and ask for immediate relief.
>
> I would have done so before, but had reason to believe that the monthly issue of Controller's warrants would be given me, which having been withheld, has caused the greatest distress.
>
> I need hardly inform the Legislature that the largest amount of appropriation which I have realized since I took the contract has been expended on improvements in the prison grounds, in wharves, grading, buildings, etc., which the State Prison committee have just said "should have been constructed long since," this showing the absolute necessity for this work.
>
> I make the foregoing statement to show that the money I have received has been properly spent, and for improvements that were absolutely necessary.

In connection with the above, it is my duty to say that instead of receiving ten thousand dollars, in accordance with the contract, I was required to accept bonds payable in twenty years, since which time they have been pronounced unconstitutional.

Being compelled to hypothecate these bonds, in order to raise money necessary to carry on the improvements, and at the same time feed, clothe, and guard the convicts, I gradually found myself surrounded with great pecuniary difficulties, arising from demands made by the depreciation of the bonds, and the heavy interest I was forced to pay for the use of the money, which was two and a half and three percent per month, and which obligations are still owing.

Following these troubles the Attorney General gave it as his opinion that the contract I had made with the State was unconstitutional. This was the "last grain of sand." It was published from the center to the circumference of the State, and the credit of the institution was wholly prostrated. Prostrated too, at a time when I was just congratulating myself that the heavy expenses connected with the improvements I was about finishing would place me in a condition to hire out most of the convicts, and I would begin to recover from the heavy outlay so necessary at the commencement of a large contract like this.

In addition to this loss with the State, given to my credit by the opinion of the Attorney General (which opinion I must do him the justice to say he has nearly or quite abandoned), I find the Board of Examiners have refused to pay the account for the support of the prison due as per contract on the last day of February.

Under the circumstances I deem it my duty to inform your honorable body that the officers, guards, and convicts are all in a suffering condition and unless immediate relief is afforded by the State I cannot answer for the result.

The expenses of the prison are about $300 per day. The debt incurred since the last day of February, [is] about $3,000; I have promised should be paid out of the first money obtained. It will take $6,000 to support the institution to the last day of this month. The warrants must be sold for what they will bring, as the Board of Examiners exhausted the last dollar belonging to the general fund by ordering over $16,000 paid to the contractor for buildings connected with the State Asylum at Stockton.

In passing a bill for the relief of the State Prison, I do not wish it worded in such a manner as to have a bearing on the contract made between the State and myself; but entirely independent of it, with the liberty on the part of the State to credit it on that contract, or refuse, at her option.

In conclusion, permit me to call the earnest attention of the Legislature to this important subject, so that immediate relief can be afforded to the convicts who have been confined by order of the State and who are consequently unable to procure it for themselves.

I am, with great respect,

—J. M. Estell
Lessee, State Prison
Sacramento, March 10, 1857

By a hurry-up legislation a bill was passed for the relief of San Quentin Prison in the sum of $25,000, payable in cash, and chargeable against Estell's lease. Thus the emergency was temporarily tided over.

15.

ADMINISTRATION OF THE STATE'S AFFAIRS FROM 1850 TO 1861 WAS SO CROOKED THAT THE ADMINISTRATIONS OF LATER BOSSES SHINE LIKE THE EFFORTS OF DISTINTERESTED AND PATRIOTIC CITIZENS

It is the nature of men to become indifferent to anything that is customary, familiar, and usual. That is the reason why sin thrives so luxuriantly in this wicked world. During a long period of my ill-spent life I delved more or less deeply into a mire of politics, and became in fact much better than a novice at the game. It was the golden era of bosses, machines, programmers, and performers, now as extinct as the mastodon and all but forgotten today. My blunted sensibilities blinded me to much that moralists would not approve in the present generation, though, in cool retrospect of old age, I must confess that we old sinners put some tough things over. But in rummaging for this story through various channels, I have incidentally unearthed so much that was hopelessly crooked, sordid, and mean in the history of California from 1850 to 1861, that the bosses, machines, programmers, and performers of the later day shine by comparison like enlightened patriots. Yea, the latter day boss looks like a saint with harp in hand and a halo around his head.

I will illustrate by one little narrative—how Governor J. Neely Johnson blackmailed Lansing Mizner—father of the famous Mizner boys—out of the cheap sum of $500. I will say as a preface that all of the statements herein made are backed up by documentary evidence.

At that point of our history there was an officer known as State Gauger of Wines and Spirits, who drew down a comfortable salary. Governor Johnson appointed Lansing Mizner to this office, and by a gentleman's agreement, it was understood that His Excellency should name the two deputy gaugers. In due season two names were presented to the gauger for appointment. According to an extant letter of Mr. Mizner, he found one of these parties, E. Rigg, "a perfect gentleman." The other, R. N. Berry, on the contrary, proved to be an unscrupulous scalawag, who had imposed on the Governor by pretending to have been a Law and Order man during the recent vigilante muss in San Francisco; whereas, in verity, he had been a shameless vigilante. For this and other sufficient reasons Mr. Mizner turned him down. For his contumacy the Governor removed the gauger from office. That is to say, when the Legislature met and it was in order to present names to the Senate for confirmation, His Excellency withdrew that of Mr. Mizner and substituted the name of another party, George W. Ryder, who was finally confirmed, leaving the late incumbent out in the cold unofficial world. In the meantime, however, the Governor had already stung his friend "Lance Mizner," as he affectionately called him, to the tune of $500, and was hard on his luck for another $500. It appears that Berry had made demand on Mizner in the Governor's name and behalf, for one-half of the proceeds of the gauger's office. The documentary evidence follows:

> State of California, Executive Department,
> Sacramento, May 26th, 1856
> L. B. Mizner, Esq.
>
> Dear Sir:
>
> I wish you to appoint R. N. Berry and Captain Edward Rigg deputy gaugers. Berry is perfectly well qualified for the duties and can be of great service to you. He is (and was when I wanted them) a staunch friend of mine, is very poor and has a family dependent upon him for support, and has not asked me

for office himself, but simply wants this position, which I assured him I would secure him. Captain Rigg is also a firm friend of mine and a reliable man. In times past he had experience and knowledge of this business. I remain truly your friend,

—J. Neely Johnson

During the immediately ensuing months Governor J. Neely Johnson's time was principally concerned in an attempt to crush the vigilance committee in San Francisco. In the fall he got his second wind. As will be remembered, Mizner had appointed Rigg, but turned Berry down. His Excellency was dissatisfied. Witness the following letter:

State of California, Executive Department, Sacramento, September 25th, 1856.

Friend Lance:

Tomorrow I leave here with my wife for Napa Springs, where I will remain for a few days. I am desirous of seeing you in reference to Dick Berry, and as I cannot go to San Francisco I wish you would meet me there on Saturday or Sunday. I hope you will take your wife with you. I want William to go up also; I will write to him to this effect. I have suggested this course so we can all meet together to arrange what shall be done for Dick. I will be there likewise.

Your friend,
J. Neely Johnson

One result of the conference at Napa Springs was the execution of the following promissory note:

San Francisco, Cal.
Sept. 30, 1856.

Six months after date I promise to pay to Wm. Neely Johnson, on order, Five Hundred Dollars, with 3½ percent per month interest, until paid, for value received interest payable from date.

L. B. Mizner

(Wm. Neely Johnson and J. Neely Johnson, Indorsers.)

Also the following receipt from Dick Berry:

Received—San Francisco, October 1, 1856, of L. B. Mizner the sum of Five Hundred Dollars, in full for an allowance of One Hundred Dollars per month for the months of October, November, and December, 1856, and January and February 1857.

R. N. Berry

Then Dick wanted more, as the following letter indicates:

San Francisco, November 1856.

Dear Governor:

I had supposed that our payment of $500—blackmail to Berry—would at least let us off for five months. But with the tenacity usually incident to one who is attempting to accomplish a contemptible end, this man Berry has had the impudence to draw on me for $100, after getting my note for $500, and then attempting to undermine me with you by writing the malicious letter he did.

My understanding with you was to pay Berry $100 per month and draw on you for $50 of it. As his "Things" were in pawn, we advanced $500, which I thought to be in full settlement for five months and he so receipted to me.

I want it distinctly understood that the $500 note was made by me solely to accommodate you, as I would not give Berry a dollar scarcely to save his life, as I look upon him as does this community, in the light of a blackguard. I know he has grossly imposed upon you. In the first place he presented himself to you as having been a strong Law and Order man, when I know of my own knowledge that he was a strong sympathizer of the V.C., for as such I had several arguments with him. Secondly, he cannot be as poor as he presents, for I am credibly informed he has bet from $200 to $500 on the election. I consider Berry as meddling with my affairs. His demand on me in your name for one-half my office was in bad faith to you and insolent to me; and I now regret that I did not kick him down the stairs, as I certainly will do if he ever enters my office again with similiar documents, or interferes in my affairs in any matter whatsoever.

Now, my dear sir, I hope you will excuse anything amiss in this letter. I am willing to do anything in my power to aid you and you can under all circumstances count on me as a faithful friend.

Your release of me from all obligations was the cause of my making permanent arrangements at a higher figure by $150 per month than could otherwise have been made. My income from the office is now such that I cannot afford to fool it away.

My respects to your wife,

Yours truly,
L. B. Mizner

P.S. As this letter most concerns Mr. Berry I have furnished him with a copy.

Feelings became more and more strained between Mizner and the Governor after the receipt of the above letter. During the latter part of March, on reliable information that the Governor proposed to withdraw the gauger's name from confirmation by the Senate, Mizner made a hurried trip to Sacramento. He was a big, two-fisted man, and his favorite fighting weight was 260 pounds. The Governor had no stomach for a personal interview and quietly holed up. The following correspondence explains itself:

Sacramento, April 1, 1857.
Hon. J. Neely Johnson:

I have now been in the city three days, and as yet have been unable to see you, notwithstanding your promise (sent by the bearer of my note yesterday) that you would see me sometime during the afternoon.

I am at a loss to know why you deny me the privilege of an interview, and shall consider your further silence in the matter as leaving me at liberty to take such steps in the promises, independent of the Executive, as may best subserve my own interests and protect my rights as an Officer and a citizen. Regretting exceedingly that my duty to myself compels me to write you this note, I have the honor to be,

Respectfully,
L. B. Mizner

On April 3rd Johnson sent in to the Senate the name of George W. Ryder, vice Mizner, withdrawn. Mizner came back as follows:

Sacramento, April 3, 1857

Sir:

Your attempt to remove me from office today has caused much excitement among my friends, who think that it casts an imputation on my character, and that supposition may be entertained that I have committed some indiscretion sufficiently great to put me properly under the ban of Executive displeasure.

In view of these facts, and to the end that my friends and the public should know the true cause of your attempts to supersede me, I shall place before the Senate, in connection with my commission, your letters asking aid for Berry, your indorsement for $500, and your separate bond for me to pay one-half of it, together with a statement of the attempt of you and Berry to obtain one-half of the proceeds of my office; that having failed, the attempt to get $100 per month and afterwards $50 per month.

I conceive this to be necessary for the protection of my own reputation and I will do it for that purpose only, distinctly disavowing any other object. I have the honor to be,

Respectfully,
L. B. Mizner

In answer to the charges preferred by Mr. Mizner, Governor Johnson appeared before a committee charged to report upon the confirmation of his new appointee, George W. Ryder, and to hear testimony regarding the foregoing facts. His Excellency, with noble candor, admitted the substantial truth of the various allegations. In explanation he stated that he was a poor man and had involved himself pecuniarily by his campaign for Governor, that he naturally expected his appointees or their deputies to relieve him from his money embarrassments, that he had made a satisfactory arrangement concerning the deputy gaugers, but Mizner had refused to appoint Berry, and the "perfect gentleman," Rigg, had reneged financially after receiving his job. Therefore, in self defense he had been compelled to have recourse to Gauger Mizner for the full sum of $1,000, of which $500 had already been paid in the form of a promissory note, which had been cashed by a bank, but not until he had compelled to endorse it personally, so that he might ultimately be forced to pay it himself, interest and all. In attempting to recover the second $500 Mizner had thrown off the mask, disclosing himself in his true character of an ingrate and tightwad. For this reason he had properly withdrawn his name for the position of gauger and substituted that of George W. Ryder, wherein he felt fully satisfied.

And so was everyone else. Governor Johnson was praised as an honorable man striving to meet his just debts, and Mizner as a contemptible squeeze who placed the dollar mark above friendship.

Here is what the Senate committee had to say:

> Mr. President:
>
> The undersigned, a majority of the committee to whom was referred the message of the Governor, appointing Geo. W. Ryder to the office of Gauger of Wines and Liquors of the City of San Francisco, have had the same under consideration and report.
>
> The committee have taken the testimony of such witnesses as would possibly throw

any light upon the subject, which is herewith filed for the consideration of the Senate.

Further, that in the opinion of the undersigned there was no evidence introduced that shows any official corruption on the part of the Executive.

(Signed) J. G. M'Callum
S. A. Merritt
C. Westmoreland

The two minority Senators remained mute.

16.

GENERAL ESTELL, AFTER MANY REVERSES, SUBLETS PRISON TO A NEW CONTRACTOR, WHO MAKES MONEY OUT OF THE EXPLOITATION OF CONVICT LABOR, BUT WHO NEGLECTS THE PRISONERS

Estell had other than financial troubles to deal with in the session of 1857. For one thing, two of his State Prison Commissioners, Controller Whitman and Treasurer Bates, were being impeached by the Legislature on charges of maleficence in office, not in connection with their management of San Quentin, but with respect to other offenses. Thus he was deprived of their official aid and support.

An Assembly committee had visited San Quentin, and utterly deceived by the apparent prospects of a large immediate profit from manufacturing projects, had reported that the prison could be run with a monthly profit to the State of $4,700. In view of the former sad experience, the solons were somewhat loath to repeat the experiment of direct State control, but in view of the opinion of Attorney General William T. Wallace that the second lease to Estell was void, the Assembly, departing entirely from its legislative functions, advertised for bids for a new contract of four years, along the lines of the Estell lease. The committee's report of prospective profits had unduly boomed the value of this doubtful property. Many bids were received and opened. Without the color of any authority a lease was actually executed by the Assembly in favor of Curtis & Denver, who were by no means the lowest bidders. But Estell's luck did not entirely desert him. Attorney General Wallace advised the Assembly that their act in leasing to Curtis & Denver was unconstitutional, null, and void.

Moreover, he changed his opinion about the Estell lease, which he finally decided to be a valid contract, only voidable by the courts on the proof of breaches of the terms by the lessee. So the Legislature adjourned with Estell still holding the fort.

But he had accumulated a fine stomach full of trouble and financial loss in the years of his connection with San Quentin Prison. Thanks to the boon report of the Assembly committee, the lease was regarded by speculators as an extremely valuable property. While the bloom was on the rose Estell decided to get out from under. While the situation was favorable he executed a transfer of all his rights under the second lease to John F. McCauley on May 14, 1857.

The consideration of this document was that McCauley should split with Estell 50-50 the ten thousand dollars received monthly from the State. In other words, if all went well, during the remaining four years of the lease Estell had coming to him the comfortable sum of $240,000, which would probably have balanced accounts. I guess in making this transfer the lessee knew that the sands of life were ebbing low. Small doubt remains that the pecuniary losses sustained, the constant anxiety, and the continued bad faith of the State broke down a rugged constitution far ahead of time. Long before his agreement with Mr. McCauley expired, James M. Estell died.

John F. McCauley took possession of the prison immediately after the signing and recalling of the above sublease, which can be found in the office of the Recorder of Marion County *Book "B."* McCauley was a forceful, determined man, not much of a humanitarian or a philanthropist, who cut his cloth in the management of the prison according to the money there was in it.

The manufacturing department proved highly profitable; the market for stone and brick in San Francisco was resilient and brisk, and everything pointed to four years of unexampled prison prosperity. I wish I could say the same of prison management. It was rotten; McCauley simply ran wild. He paid no attention whatsoever to the Board of State Prison Commissioners.

He erected no new buildings, although called upon to do so by the Board. The prisoners were poorly fed, only two indifferent meals a day, and left almost entirely unclad. He continued the trusty system; exercised his assumed right to engage convicts in profitable projects away from the prison. Punishments became more frequent and severe, especially among those working in the mechanical department, who were flogged for laziness at the whim of their superiors. Liquor was sold within the prison lines. I think, but am not sure, that open gambling became habitual at this time, a practice that endured long after the State took charge of the institution.

Naturally enough, McCauley brought up a hornet's nest about his care. On January 9, 1858, a joint legislative committee visited San Quentin and handed back a bird of a report to the solons at Sacramento. It opens with the following picture of the old prison, which should be of interest to the present generation:

> The prison buildings are enclosed by a wall some twenty feet in height and of sufficient width apparently to give the strength required so as to answer the purposes for which it was intended, the east wall being in length 500 feet, the west wall 500 feet, the south wall 600 feet and the north wall 524 feet, with an entrance from the east and west into the enclosed yard or grounds about midway of said east and west walls. The entrance on the west has a good, substantial

iron door or gate, while the one on the east, which is the main entrance, has but little more than a common wooden door and could not be considered a serious obstacle in the way of prisoners wishing to make their escape.

The prison building is situated within the yard and is at the left of the east entrance and in size 180 feet in length east and west, 24 feet in width north and south, and in height two stories, the upper or second being divided into forty-eight cells 6 by 10⅓ feet each, opening to the outside of the building, there being a kind of balcony or corridor around the second story unto which you ascend by a flight of stairs at the east end of the building. Twenty-eight feet of the east end of the lower story is separated from the remainder by a partition and used as a hospital. The remaining 146 feet is in one room and designated as the long room. About halfway between the east and west walls of the prison yard is a building one story in height, some 200 feet in lenght north and south by 34 feet in width, 19 feet of the north being used as a tailor shop, adjoining which is 41 feet used as a kitchen; 17 feet of the south part is divided into two rooms and is occupied by the female prisoners, adjoining which is a division of 34 feet named the county jail.

The remaining 134 feet is used as a dining room. Immediately adjoining and to the west of the above described building is a building one story in height, some 400 feet in length by 30 feet in width, subdivided into six divisions used for different mechanical purposes.

Outside the prison walls but immediately adjoining the east entrance, are some new brick buildings (not understood to be upon the property belonging to the State, and known as personal property), which very much add to the comfort of the lessee and those employed by him, which buildings were not built by or under the direction of the State Prison Commissioners, but that the lessee took down other buildings belonging to the State and now uses the new ones in their stead. After which explanation of the prison grounds, wall and buildings, we requested John F. McCauley, who claimed to represent the lessee, to cause all the prisoners to be assembled in the dining room and the roll called, each prisoner as his name should be called to pass out of the room, which request was promptly and apparently cheerfully complied with.

The roll being called, five hundred and six answered to their names as called, leaving according to the prison books ten not accounted for, of which number not answering to their names and not being at the prison, the committee ascertained the following, *viz.*: Evans (alias Texas Jack), Jackway, and Butts lived at some place on a ranch (Fairfax Home, J.H.W.); Morton at Mr. Simms', San Rafael; Gilman at Stocker's Ranch; and an Indian girl with Mrs. McCauley at San Francisco—all outside the prison precincts. A convict named Riley died January 19, 1858, whose name still remained on the books and should be deducted from the ten not answering their names at the roll call, which would leave three not accounted for—the books requiring in all the full number of five hundred and fifteen under sentence and confined at the prison, while only five hundred six answered at the prison, six being at different places outside the prison precincts, and three missing and unaccounted for entirely.

In addition to the testimony of witnesses, as above referred to, the committee would state, that from personal observation and examination, they found on the 19th of January, the evening of their arrival at the prison, some one hundred and twenty prisoners entirely barefoot, and quite a number with nothing more than old gunnysacks or pieces of blankets tied around their feet, none having anything in the shape of socks furnished them by the lessee. It is due however, to the lessee, or Mr. McCauley who claims to represent him, that on the next day quite a number of the barefoot party of the day before came out with new shoes, Mr. McCauley stating that many of the prisoners had concealed or hid away their shoes, so as to look as badly as possible, but the committee, although visiting every apartment within the walls of the prison, failed to discover the secret place where were concealed the missing shoes of the shoeless prisoners, although the committee does not undertake to state positively that such secret place may not be in existence, and may be hereafter discovered by the closer scrutiny of more interested parties. The general clothing of the prisoners seems too scant for winter weather; the most of their clothing, or a great proportion thereof, appears to be the last remains of what was worn there by them, now in such a tattered, torn, forbidding, and filthy condition, that the commmonest street beggars sleeping by the wayside and begging their daily bread, would by comparison have the appearance of newly Parisian clad gentlemen.

The report goes on to state that the sleeping quarters were filthy, lousy, ill-provided with any adequate kind of covering, and drew a horrifying picture of overcrowding, which was equally true thirty years after, to my own knowledge—such had been the wanton indifference of the State.

The Committee had McCauley on the carpet for something like twenty counts. The lease once more was declared unconstitutional, null, and void. By a provision of the old constitution the State could not run in debt for more than $300,000. The second Estell lease providing for payments of $10,000 a month for five years must be considered in its entirety, argued the committee, making a total of $600,000. Therefore the instrument was doubly null and void. Despite the constitutional restraint, the State had issued a bonded debt of nearly $4,000,000, the constitutionality of which was under review. Under all the circumstances the committee advised that the State take immediate charge of San Quentin Prison, after ejecting the present interlopers.

17.

STATE AGAIN TAKES CONTROL OF THE PRISON AFTER THE LESSEE HAS BEEN FORCIBLY OUSTED BY ORDER OF THE LEGISLATURE, BUT THE COURTS STEP IN TO PROTECT THE RIGHTS OF McCAULEY

The argument of the Joint Investigating Committee that the Estell lease was null and void because of the constitutional provision limiting the debt that the State might incur to $300,000 was fortified by an opinion of Attorney General Thomas H. Williams to the same effect, not withstanding the opinion of ex-Attorney General Wallace to the contrary. The Legislature then proceeded to enact a law creating a new Board of Prison Directors: the Governor of the State, the Lieutenant Governor, and the Secretary of State, arming them with plenary powers to administer the affairs of the State Prison at San Quentin, to appoint a warden, establish rules, and take immediate posession of the property. The sub-lessee was allowed three months in which to remove his personal property. The sum of $75,000 a year was appropriated for the support of the prison. Meanwhile the allowance of $10,000 a month to McCauley automatically ceased. The old Board of Prison Commissioners was abolished.

Prior thereto, in view of the disclosure of the Joint Investigating Committee, the Legislature had passed an emergency act, simply directing the Governor to take immediate possession of the State Prison at San Quentin.

McCauley entered a vigorous protest to Governor Weller at this summary dismissal of himself without regard to his rights or compensation. He pointed out that if the lease of 1856 to Estell was null and void, then the settlements with Estell for large sums of money, recognized in said lease and made a part thereof, were equally void. The situation opened up the way for endless litigation. He was ready to adjust all claims, both of Estell and himself, on very reasonable terms, and he implored His Excellency to call the attention of the Legislature to this vital defect in their procedure.

This the Governor did, and very earnestly. In a special message he drew attention to the great importance of settling all disputes before the State took over the management of the State Prison. But the Legislature with its usual fatuous policy believed it could sidestep its unquestioned obligations, and it again succeeded in placing an enormous obligation on the neck of the suffering State. The defendants seemed to have been desperately afraid of County Judge R. B. Frink, before whom the case was to be tried. They charged his honor with bias and asked for a change of venue, which Frink promptly denied.

Judge Frink tried the case and his judgment was a sweeping victory for the plaintiff. The judgment ordered immediate restitution of the State Prison property and gave in addition a judgment against John B. Weller for $12,299.93 and $288 costs. This judgment against Weller covered only one month of unlawful detainer, and similar damages would accrue monthly if the decision held good. Walkup and Foreman were discharged as far as money damages were concerned.

About this time it came to be known publicly that the power behind the McCauley throne was no other than Lloyd Tevis. This gentleman had already laid the foundation for his vast financial wealth, and also for the peculiar political influence that he exercised for many years behind the drop curtain. Just a handful of the elect knew the extent of his silent power, and learned to recognize in his perennial smile either a benediction or a death warrant.

The general reputation of Lloyd Tevis then—which only deepened as time flowed on—was that he never failed to get what he went after. Up to this time his name had not been mentioned in the litigation, but the established fact that he was financially interested in it had a most depressing effect on Governor Weller and the official family at San Quentin Prison.

Another suit brought related to the real property at San Quentin Prison. As will be remembered, the State bought twenty acres from B. R. Buckalew, the original site of the prison. This was part of the unconfirmed Spanish grant known as the Punta de Quentín. In the possible event of failure to confirm, Estell, with the knowledge and consent of the Prison Inspectors, had filed a homestead claim against the property, and if the Rancho failed of confirmation, Estell's title to the twenty acres was perfectly good.

Again, as to the sixteen acres sold by Buckalew to Estell and others, and by them to the San Francisco Manufacturing Company to Archibald Woods, Estell's father-in-law, and by him during the year 1854 to John Bigler, Governor of California, and his successors, the various deeds seemed a complete chain of title up to the State when I searched the title. I was puzzled when this land was referred to in later official documents either as Estell's property or property in which he claimed to have an interest. But the facts are simple when explained. The consideration of $40,000 mentioned in the instrument, as usual, never had been paid by the State, and there was an unrecorded side agreement that, until this sum had been paid, that State only had an easement in the property, voidable in the event of non-payment.

McCauley, in Estell's name, brought suits to quiet title to each of these properties. He actually recovered judgment in the lower court for the sixteen acres, which gave him title not only to the brickyard and wharf, but also to quite a strip of the enclosed property, including the entire west wall of the prison.

18.

McCAULEY, THE LESSEE, HAS TRIUMPHANT ENTRY TO SAN QUENTIN, AFTER THE COURTS DECIDED HIS DISPOSSESSION WAS NOT LEGAL, AND THE STATUTE WAS UNCONSTITUTIONAL

Of course an appeal was taken from Judge Frink's decision to the Supreme Court, where as a summary proceeding it had the right-of-way. The Supreme Court as then constituted had a membership of three. The incumbents were David S. Terry, Chief Justice, Stephen J. Field, and J. G. Baldwin, Associates. Concerning Terry and Field, whatever may be the estimate of their career as men, history has justly given them a secure place as great lawyers. Judge Baldwin was also as able a man as ever adorned the bench. His life came to a tragic end in one of the first serious railroad accidents in California.

It was like a bolt from the blue when this learned tribunal handed down a decision affirming the judgment of Judge R. B. Frink at every point and particular. The opinion was written by Chief Justice Terry, and concurred in by Judge Baldwin, while Mr. Justice Field wrote a concurring decision in his masterly power of statement, giving additional point to the views of his associates. In the concluding paragraph he takes an awful fall, in a way of gentle sarcasm, out of Attorney General Williams. The decision is historic in settling various vexed questions. It can be found on Page 500, Vol. 12, *Cal. Reports*, and embraces thirty-six pages.

All of it is good reading, but it is only possible to reproduce the following syllabus of the opinion:

> Forcible Entry and Detainer. Action Construed. The action of forcible entry and detainer is a summary proceeding to recover possession of premises forcibly or unlawfully detained. The inquiry is confined in such cases to the actual peacable possession of the plaintiff and the unlawful or forcible ouster or detention by defendant—the object of the law being to prevent the disturbance of the public peace by the forcible assertion of a private right. Question of title or right of posession cannot arise; a forcible entry upon the actual posession of plaintiff being proven, he would be entitled to restitution, though the fee simple, title, and present right of posession is known to be in the defendant.
>
> Forcible Entry Defined.—Where the Governor of the State, who is authorized and it is made his duty by law, to take immediate possession of the State Prison and grounds then in the possession of a lessee of the State, goes in company with other officers of State upon the grounds of the Prison, and demands of the person in charge the keys of the prison, which being refused, the door of the room in which the keys were was forced by order of the Governor and the keys taken, and thus the posession of the Prison and ground taken by the Governor in the name and on behalf of the State; Hold, that such acts amounted to a forcible entry on the part of the Governor, and he is personally liable therefore. Further hold, that the acts of the Governor warranted the conclusion that any attempt on the part of the lessee to resume possession of the prison would be resisted by force.

Compensation Before Condemnation.—Although the State possess the constitutional power to take private property for public purposes, by providing just compensation therefore, yet the means of compensating the owner must be provided before the property is taken.

Statute Invalid.—The act of February the twenty-sixth 1858, under which the Governor justified the taking, made no provision for compensation, and is therefore, clearly in violation of Section 8 of Article I of the Constitution of the State.

Issues in Action.—The validity of the lease under which the lessee held the premises cannot be tried in the action, nor can the lessee be deprived of the advantages resulting from the possession of the premises under the lease, by a forcible ouster under legislative enactment.

Injunction to Restrain Enforcement of Statute.—Assuming the lease to have been valid, there was in the plaintiff a property of which he could not be divested for public use without just compensation. His right so far as the land and buildings were concerned was in no respect affected by the fact that they were designed as a place for the confinement of convicts. The purposes for which premises are leased cannot alter the nature of the lease holds interest as property. To take such property without compensation is beyond the reach of legislative power. Such compensation must be made, or a fund provided from which it can be made in advance. So strictly is this rule adhered to that the enforcement of any statute to take such property, where the indemnity has not been provided, will be stayed by injunction.

> Statute Unconstitutional—An act of the Legislature appropriating private property without providing compensation is unconstitutional and void. It may not be absolutely essential that the compensation should be provided in the same act which authorizes the seizure, but is essential that it should be provided before the seizure can be enforced or justified.
>
> Forfeiture of Lease From State—How Asserted—The Governor cannot rest his justification in taking the premises upon any possible forfeiture of the lease under which plaintiff held. Such forfeiture cannot be asserted except by force of a judicial determination. The Legislature cannot take upon itself, nor the officers of the government upon themselves, to adjudge what is right as accrued to the State, and then proceed to enforce it, any more than a private citizen.

Governor Weller, Attorney General Williams, and other officials of the State concerned were completely stunned by the sweeping decision of the Supreme Court. To the Governor himself it was a body blow, indeed. He found himself suddenly confronted with a personal judgment for $12,322.49, with a certainty that he would be held responsible for ten times that sum additional whenever McCauley saw fit to bring suit for his monthly damages. Already he was responsible for the considerable sum of $135,552.89, besides the cost bill in Judge Frink's court, amounting to $238.08, and a much larger bill in the Supreme Court, not yet assessed. As the before mentioned claims would bear interest at the high current rate then allowed by law, as each became due monthly, it will be seen that Governor Weller had judgments present and prospective hanging over his head to the tune of at least $150,000. All of this was not conducive to the peace and tranquility of the executive slumbers. The forceful nature of the Supreme Court decision made a petition for a hearing an absolute waste of time, and, moreover, Weller was losing money by his unlawful detainer at the rate of $400 a day. Nevertheless a rehearing was asked for. It was all in the nature of sparring for time which Weller utilized in memorials and even supplications to the Legislature to enact laws, such as would enable the State to make a final settlement with McCauley, protect the executive from great personal losses, and retain the San Quentin Prison in possession of the State. But the Legislature dawdled away its time.

The law's delays were exhausted and on Saturday, April 14, 1858, McCauley came back to his own. I am sorry to say that McCauley was not a generous or magnanimous victor. Good winners are few and far between—far rarer indeed than good losers. Poor old Warden Walkup wished to walk down in a stately, ceremonious way, but McCauley would have none of it. He came over from San Francisco on a chartered ferry boat, with a full official list, a number of invited guests, and a brass band. The procession formed on the wharf at San Quentin Point, the band playing the melody, "We'll all get drunk, when Johnny comes marching home."

Many voices joined in the refrain. Next came McCauley with the eminent Marin County jurist, Judge Frink, on his right, whose decision the Supreme Court had just affirmed, and Chief Counsel A. P. Crittenden on his left. Distinguished invited guests followed, and what might be called a life saving corps, with demijohns, case goods, and solid refreshments, brought up the rear.

Warden Walkup and his officers were drawn up at the front gate of the prison ready to turn over the works officially when the rather odd procession approached. The Lieutenant-Governor, as Warden, stepped forward, and presented the keys, which McCauley accepted rather ungraciously. Then the restored potentate had a word to say "for the good of the order." McCauley did not have the intellectual powers of his great English namesake, but possessed a rough gift of speech and a wicked tongue. Addressing the rival assemblages he recounted in detail the long story of his wrongs—how he had been set upon and despoiled by a combination of pirates, porch-climbers, and horse thieves, but through the courage and high acumen of the judiciary—and here the speaker glanced significantly at Judge Frink—their plans had been frustrated and he had come back triumphantly to his own. Then, turning to the late officials, he remarked, "You get, and don't let me see your ugly mugs around my prison again!"

Everyone, except the dismissed officials, gave three cheers for "Johnny McCauley." The convicts, who had thronged to the main gate, with the enthusiasm of their kind for any old change, turned loose a mighty shout and the band played "Annie Laurie." McCauley, touched by the enthusiasm of the inmates, went inside the yard and delivered an address to the convicts, conjuring them to believe that Johnny McCauley was their sincere well-wisher and friend. The prisoners' hilarity was further heightened by an order for free distribution of grog and the promise of a bang-up Sunday dinner.

It was a red-letter day for San Quentin Prison. Refreshments, both solid and liquid, had been prepared on such a liberal scale that a considerable contingent from San Rafael, scenting the wassail from afar, were gladly welcomed to the feast. Everyone acquired something nice, all the way from a souse to a fist fight.

The San Franciscans returned home late in the afternoon. Over the calm waters of the Bay, as the specially chartered ferry boat rounded Angel Island, floated the voluptuous strains of dance music by the band, indicating that the returning guests were still having a fairly good time of it.

No, I was not there myself, nor is the story of McCauley's return to San Quentin Prison obtainable from any printed or written record. But when I moved to San Rafael in 1862, how McCauley came back to San Quentin Prison was still a recent and verdant memory.

I have heard the story repeated by eyewitnesses of undoubted credibility, such as Dr. A. W. Taliaferro; from John Simms, then my neighbor across the street, who had a contract for supplying beef to the prison and who acted as McCauley's representative when Weller rejected him, and who acted as a kind of master of ceremonies when he returned; from Dan Taylor, long time County Clerk; and lastly from Judge Frink, who took a pardonable pride in his part of making history. While I may have added a daub of color here and there, the story is, in all material respects, precisely as it was told to me by the above named witnesses.

19.

THE LEGISLATURE IN ITS EFFORT TO OUST THE LESSEE OF THE PRISON, GETS INTO A FURTHER TANGLE FROM WHICH THEY TRY TO FREE THEMSELVES BY OFFERING THE OLIVE BRANCH

For the sake of sequence, it may be well to follow up here to the end the legislative acts and negotiations growing out of the lease to Estell of 1856, and his subsequent sale or sublease to McCauley. In spite of Governor Weller's frantic appeal, the Legislature of 1859 did absolutely nothing in the way of permanent settlement. In spite, also, of the stern rebuke received from the Supreme Court, solons again tried to oust McCauley by indirection. An act was passed requiring the Attorney General to immediately institute a suit in the District Court of the Seventh Judicial District and condemn thirty-six acres at Point San Quentin, otherwise known as State Prison property. It was a bird of a law. All the rights of a defendant in such cases made and provided were cast to the winds.

This act recognized to some extent the faulty nature of the State's title, but the real design was to steal a roundabout march on McCauley. By its terms, a judgment could be obtained in less than sixty days. The jury, in basing damages, was to consider only the value of adjacent land and allow nothing for value of site or of its value to the State. Upon the rendering of a verdict by the jury, the Sheriff was instructed to put the State in possession of the property immediately, expelling at the same time other interlopers. After he was ousted thus, the defendant was graciously allowed the right to appeal to the Supreme Court.

This legislation was so flagrantly in defiance of all law and precedent that the Attorney General, Thomas H. Williams, who had not been consulted concerning its passage, indignantly refused to father it in an enlightened court of justice.

Having lost faith in the Attorney General, it would seem the employment of able counsel was directed by the legislature to test the validity of the contract of 1856. As such a line of litigation, not being summary, would require many years for its final adjustment, McCauley only jeered.

McCauley had the whole State government buffaloed. He only had to mention what "me and Tevis" would do to a recalcitrant official to make that official lick the dust at his feet. He took out executions against Governor Weller and employed bill collectors to dog his footsteps. He compelled the State Controller to resume the issuance of warrants in his favor to the extent of $10,000 a month, and the Treasurer paid them. He referred to San Quentin as "my prison" or "my property," and talked as if his grip on the realty would continue his authority forever and amen.

Governor Weller, in his final message to the Legislature, referred with deep feeling to the San Quentin situation. He mentioned the grievous complications in which he found himself personally involved by obeying the mandate of the Legislature. He regretted that he had not the remotest idea what McCauley was doing with San Quentin Prison and its inmates, because the indignities that the sublease had heaped upon himself and the other prison directors made it impossible with regard to their self-respect to visit any place under his charge. He again urged a final and complete settlement of all claims against the State, which were almost daily becoming more complicated.

Finally, after much deliberation, the following act, which I take the liberty of quoting in full, was introduced. I may state in advance that it was not the settlement made. The State of California and Messrs. McCauley and Tevis disagreed on the important question of cash.

The People of the State of California, represented in Senate and Assembly, do enact as follows:

(Approved April 20, 1860)

1. The Governor, Attorney General, and State Treasurer are hereby appointed a Board of Commissioners, with authority and power to compromise and settle with John F. McCauley and Lloyd Tevis, assigneess of James M. Estell, deceased, all claims against the State of California held by them or either of them, and arising out of, or in any manner connected with, the contract made on the 26th day of March, 1856, between the State of California, by Robert M. Anderson, Lieutenant-Governor, George W. Whitman, Controller, and Henry Bates, Treasurer of the State, composing the Board of State Prison Commissioners, of the one part, and the said James M. Estell of the other part, for a lease of the State Prison and convict labor for a term of five years.

2. The said Commissioners shall have power to make such compromise and settlement upon the following terms and conditions, and not otherwise:

First—That the said McCauley and Tevis shall release the State from all claims and demands whatsoever, for any and all sums of money due or to become due under said contract, or for any violation thereof; that they shall consent to the revision and cancellation of said contract, and shall deliver up to said Commissioners for the State, the State Prison convicts and all the property of the State known as the State Prison property, in their possession or the possession of either of them.

Second—That the said McCauley shall release John B. Weller, State Governor of the State of California, and all other persons who acted under his authority and direction, from all claims and demands whatsoever, for the taking and detention by him or them, at any time heretofore, of any property of the said McCauley, and shall also release the State from all claims and demands for property of the said McCauley taken by the said Weller or by any person acting under his authority, and which has not been heretofore restored to the said McCauley.

Third—The amount to be paid to said McCauley and Tevis upon such compromise and settlement, shall not exceed the sum of two hundred thousand dollars; one-half of the amount which the Commissioners may agree as due Mr. McCauley shall be paid in cash and the remainder upon the expiration of six months.

3. Upon any settlement being agreed upon under authority of this act, the said Commissioners are authorized to demand and receive from the State Controller, and said Controller is required to deliver to said Commissioners, his warrants, drawn upon the State Treasurer, payable to the order of said Commissioners, in such sums as may be designated by said Commissioners, not to exceed in the aggregate the sum of two hundred thousand dollars; provided that not more than one-half of said warrants shall be payable immediately, and the balance thereof shall be payable six months after their date, and it shall be expressed on their face; and the said Commissioners are authorized to endorse said warrants in blank, and upon the surrender to them of the State Prison, State Prison convicts, and State Prison property, and the delivery to them by said McCauley and Tevis of written instruments of release, good and sufficient to carry into effect the terms of the compromise, the said Commissioners are authorized to deliver said warrants to said McCauley and Tevis.

4. The Treasurer of State is hereby directed and requirer to pay all warrants drawn under the provisions of this act, whenever they shall be payable and shall be presented for payment; and for the payment thereof, the sum of one-half thereof is hereby specifically appropriated out of the general fund, and the further sum, which may be agreed upon as the balance due upon a compromise, shall be paid out of any moneys in the treasury not otherwise appropriated, and which shall not have been hertofore specifically appropriated.

5. All instruments of writing received by said Commissioners from said McCauley and Tevis shall be filed in the office of the Secretary of State.

6. The Board of Commissioners shall make a full and complete report in writing of all their proceedings and awards under this act, and submit the same to both houses of the next Legislature.

7. Whenever the settlement contemplated in this act shall be made, the State Prison, prisoners, and all the property connected therewith, shall be taken possession by the Board of Directors of the State Prison, who shall conduct the management thereof according to law.

8. This act shall take effect from and after its passage.

The good old solons, offering this olive branch in token of defeat, thought the peace offering sufficient.

20.

McCAULEY AND TEVIS, THE LESSEES OF THE PRISON, HAVING REFUSED A COMPROMISE OF $200,000 AGREE TO TAKE A LARGER SUM, WHICH THE SOLONS FINALLY AGREE TO PAY THEM

The tender of the State to settle for all its differences with Tevis and McCauley for the sum of $200,000 was promptly and indignantly rejected by those gentlemen. However, an intimation was thrown out carelessly that a raise of fifty percent, or therabouts, might serve as a basis of negotiation. Accordingly the Legislature, ten days after the passage of the first Compromise Act, passed a second Act supplementary of the former, in words and figures, to wit:

AMENDATORY OF FORMER ACT

(Approved April 30, 1860)

The People of the State of California, represented in Senate and Assembly, do enact as follows:

1. Section 2 of said act is hereby amended so as to read as follows:

2. The said Commissioners shall have power to make such compromise and settlement upon the following terms and conditions and not otherwise.

First—That the said McCauley and Tevis, shall release the State from any and all claims and demands whatever, whether in law or equity, for any and all sums of money due or to become due under said contract, for any violation thereof; that said contract shall be cancelled and rescinded and that said parties shall surrender and deliver up to said commissioners for the State the State Prison convicts, and all the property of the State known as the "State Prison Property," in their possession or in the possession of either of them, or any other person whatsoever.

Second—That the said McCauley shall release John B. Weller, late Governor of the State of California, and all other persons who acted under his authority and direction, from all claims and demands whatever, for the taking and detention by him or them, at any time heretofore, of any property of the said McCauley or Tevis, and shall also release the State from all claims and demands for any property of the said McCauley or Tevis, taken or detained by the said Weller, or by any person or persons acting under his authority, and which has not been heretofore restored to the said McCauley.

Third—That the amount to be paid to said McCauley and Tevis, upon such compromise and settlement, shall not exceed the sum of two hundred and seventy-five thousand dollars; one-half of the amount which the Commissioners may agree upon as due to said McCauley and Tevis shall be paid in cash, and the remainder upon the expiration of six months.

3. This act shall take effect from and after its passage.

Then commenced a long and tedious series of negotiations between Messrs. Tevis and McCauley and the duly appointed Commissioners of the State. Good reasons existed for dilatory proceedings. During the long summer months the lease was making money to beat the band. McCauley had a fine list of contracts for brick and stone delivery. The matter hung fire through the good old summer time until one of the commissioners, Governor John G. Downey, manifested marked symptoms of weariness. Finally on August 11, 1860, a full settlement was arrived at between the State and Messrs. Tevis and McCauley, assignees of James M. Estell, deceased. By its terms the lease was cancelled and devised to the State, and the disputed title to the thirty-six acres of prison lands was confirmed, released, devised, quit claimed, bargained, and sold to the said State of California forever. But there was a small, perhaps an insignificant, joker in the final agreement, namely, that the property was to remain in the possession of the lessee for two additional months, that is to say, until October 11, 1860, on which date the property and prisoners were to be delivered to the representatives of the State. By this shrewd arrangement, McCauley annexed the last two profitable months of the year, the period suitable for brick-making and quarrying stone. He turned over to the State the four lean months, up to the date when his contract would have expired automatically. McCauley was granted this stay of proceedings on the grounds of time necessary to wind up business. The State paid the full sum of $275,000 for the release.

On the elevation of Milton S. Latham to the Senate of the United States a few days after his inauguration as Governor, Lieutenant-Governor John G. Downey was his successor to the high office and I. N. Quinn, President of the Senate, succeeded as Lieutenant-Governor. Promptly on October 11, Quinn presented his credentials to McCauley. It was no Johnny McCauley's return feast, but the most matter of fact and commonplace ceremonial in the world. McCauley simply handed over the keys, introduced the new Warden, and took off for other parts. I should have mentioned that a legislative act had made the Lieutenant-Governor the ex-officio warden of San Quentin Prison at a salary of $250 a month and found, thus greatly enhancing the value of the job and at the same time hopelessly linking up the institution with the worst form of machine politics.

Thus ended the stormy period of the State Prison lease, lasting ten years less a little over four months, including the two disastrous epochs of the State's occupancy. Had the State, as represented by its Legislature, shown any decent regard for the discharge of its obligation under the original lease with Estell, the system might have worked fairly well temporarily, that is to say, during the formation period of the young State. On the contrary, the Legislature acted in bad faith from beginning to end, and brought the lessee to such straits that he permitted many things to be done that would not otherwise have happened. And, as fate seems to provide in all such cases, the State paid the price.

In his message to the legislature in 1861, Governor J. G. Downey, while congratulating the people on the recent acquisition of the prison property, took occasion to refer to the fact that through various acts of plain dam foolishness the State had dawdled away, according to the controller's books, the amount of $1,164,672.40 through crude, undigested experiments in prison affairs. Even leaving out the forty cents, the sum total was sufficiently large to attract attention in an already bankrupt State.

Tevis and McCauley settled with the heirs of James M. Estell according to the best traditions of punctilious business honor. The original terms of the sale might have been seriously modified, owing to the State's forcible occupancy and final curtailment of the lease. But gentlemen preferred the magnanimous course and paid 100 cents on the dollar. The Estell family became extinct in the male line, but his granddaughters, through fortunate marriages, are now numbered among the elect.

McCauley retired with a handsome fortune, which afterward increased. Nor would it be a violent inference from the foregoing facts to assume that Mr. Lloyd Tevis did not suffer financially.

This story has extended far beyond the original limit intended. It was intended to outline in compact form a narrative detail of the old prison lease; but the work as usual has spread over an unexpected area. Now, having put all the leading actors to bed and drawn down the curtains, it would seem only the decent and appropriate thing to conclude this chapter with the legend, "the end." I have seen the end appended to so much that is dear in life to me that the very word suggests an almost inexpressible sadness. For that reason, perhaps I am tempted to ask the indulgence of the reader to the extent of two, or at most, three chapters more.

21.

DURING McCAULEY'S SECOND ADMINISTRATION HE RULED SAN QUENTIN LIKE A FEUDAL LORD, DEFIED THE POWER OF THE STATE TO TAKE ANY PART IN ITS AFFAIRS, AND EVEN MADE HIS OWN LAWS

Something should be said concerning what might be called the second administration of McCauley under the San Quentin Prison lease. During the period of a year and a half, from April 14, 1859 to October 11, 1860, he was in all respects a law unto himself. He ruled like some old feudal potentate with a castle on the Rhine. Neither Governor Weller, Lieutenant-Governor Walkup, or Secretary of State Foreman, comprising the State Board of Prison Directors, visited San Quentin after his return. He let it be widely known that he would tolerate no meddling or interference. During many months of Governor Downey's administration the main effort of the State was to placate the man to an extent that would make a settlement of his claims possible. To the very day of his final retirement he was the unchallenged lord of all he surveyed.

Under such conditions, accurate information is next to impossible. From the best I can learn, there was a marked improvement in the quantity and quality of food. Three meals were served daily instead of two. But when you have said that, you have said nearly all. Punishments were frequent and severe. Convicts were worked miles from the institution, wherever a profitable job appeared. Wholesale gambling ran riot in the yard on Sundays and holidays. Hard liquor was easily obtainable by convicts who had the money to buy it. The population of the prison increased greatly, and although there was now more cell room, the horrors of overcrowding increased apace.

At the same time another vice, far more insidious than the immoderate use of alcohol and far more difficult to reach with repressive measures, gained a foothold, or to more accurate, a stronghold, from which it was not dislodged for forty years. This was the opium habit. It was introduced by the Chinese prisoners and rapidly acquired by those of other nationalities. For a time it remained practically unheeded. When the more ghastly results of the vice were made apparent, the prison authorities were virtually powerless to deal with it. The supply of opium came from the outside and traffic was immensely profitable. All sorts of leading citizens were concerned in it. Unquestionably for that reason, it was impossible for thirty years to enact a law making the introduction of opium into San Quentin a penal offense. Only after it had been declared first a misdemeanor and at last a felony were the authorities able to make any headway at all against the opium habit. Even then the underground channels remained, and daring speculators, through the lure of vast profits, were long willing to take a chance.

McCauley, in the exercise of his autocratic authority, had worked out a sort of parole scheme of his own. When he noticed a peculiarly industrious and deserving convict he had a quiet conversation with him to this effect:

> Bill, I have noticed you with an approving eye, but I am not yet satisfied with the sincerity of your reformation. But keep up the same lick for a few months longer and then I will furnish you with the facilities for making a decent getaway.

Naturally enough, with such an attractive bait before his eyes, Bill worked like a Paladin of old, and cheered on his pals to do likewise. There were always from thirty to forty such candidates on probation in the yard—that is to say, proving their worthiness to win the priceless privilege of escaping under genteel auspices. It is also needless to add that their commendable ambitions and examples had a fine tonic effect on the whole convict body. In all such side transactions, McCauley's word was as good as gold.

One of the last acts of his administration was the construction of a big brick hotel in San Rafael. It still stands on the main thoroughfare of that burg. The convict workers were confined overnight in the old adobe court house, formerly the abode of Don Timoteo Murphy. On the eve when the construction work was practically completed, the entire number, about fourteen or fifteen prisoners, picked their way through the soft adobe wall and vanished into the night, while the guards, with other congenial spirits, were exploring the mysteries of draw poker in the saloon across the way. No attempt was made to deny the report that the group was composed of McCauley's "honor men," and that their escape had been prearranged.

By holding out these illicit inducements and by sudden spasms of generosity, McCauley really managed to maintain a fair state of discipline in the yard. One of these spasms of generosity was a regular distribution of tobacco, which was withheld, however, from chronic trouble breeders. It was a coarse grade of tobacco, what was then known to the trade as "nigger-heel," but it was prized as highly by the inmates as if it had been grown in Turkey and prepared for use by the dark-eyed beauties of the Orient.

These measures, the first utterly lawless, and indefensible, showed at least basic knowledge of human nature. The discipline, as I have said, was good. No attempt whatever was made to promote a general outbreak. Escapes were plenty enough, but they were all or nearly all duly authorized and "legal." All of these redounded to the great advantage of McCauley in a financial way, through an appeal to the prisoner's strongest instinct. The lessee was at San Quentin for the money there might be in it—frankly out for the stuff—and whatever tended in that direction was conclusively expedient and right.

One result of the McCauley policy was a feeling of greater security among the inhabitants of Marin County. They were no longer quaking with alarm over the menace of desperate escaped convicts hiding in the brush in the neighborhood of their homes. The escapes now made clean getaways, usually stowing away in one of the prison boats, clad in a neat citizen's suit and stepping ashore in San Francisco like gentlemen. These opera *bouffe* escapes were never reported to the outside authorities, which simplified matters immensely. So far as Marin County went, the opinion was all but universal that McCauley was the right man in the right place.

McCauley had a staff of officers and guards, every one of whom was a picked man. Each and all of them had well-earned reputations as desperate gun fighters, as frontiersmen, rangers, and ex-deputy sheriffs in border mining towns. From them McCauley expected implicit obedience, which they frankly gave him, receiving in return fair treatment and fair pay. With these efficient guardians at the helm, it was clearly understood in convict circles that if a prisoner not eligible to escape attempted to put over any monkey business in the line of a getaway, the penalty would be swift and the transgressor would pay for it with his life.

These officers and guards were far from being saints, but were a much higher grade of men than the cheapskates and barroom bummers who succeeded them under the political administration of the State.

One shocking tragedy of the early period, as related to me by Dr. A. W. Taliaferro, for years the prison physician, I can find no trace of whatever, but my recollection of the story is clearly fixed in my memory and I believe the facts I am about to relate are true. I can only fix the dates by the fact that it must have been after several brass cannon were mounted on the rising mound to the north of the prison. This was some time during the ill-starred and short-lived period of Joseph Walkup.

The tragic event was as follows:

A number of prisoners were hurriedly loading a schooner with brick in advance of the ebb tide. A gunner at one of the posts who had been watching them narrowly, imagined he saw something suspicious in their movements and made up his mind that they were in the act of escaping. Without a moments' notice or reflection the guard got the range precisely and turned loose a quart or so of buckshot among the men. Nearly all the prisoners engaged were either killed or wounded. Dr. Taliaferro happened to be in the prison at the time; he hurried to the schooner at once and described the scene to me as frightful beyond description.

Eight or nine were killed outright and twice as many wounded. I do not vouch for this story further than as stated above.

In the matter of sanitation, McCauley had the great advantage of what was then an up-to-date hospital, constructed mainly by Walkup; therefore, the sick enjoyed better quarters and better care than in the past. Considerable improvements had been added to the cooking plant. Otherwise, the sanitary arrangements were entirely primitive. The sewer system and drainage were a shade better than nothing at all. No arrangements existed for bathing. The outside appearance of the institution was unclean and forbidding. The cells and dormitories were "crummy," that is to say, infested with bed bugs, fleas, and lice.

Some contemporary criminologists were wont to describe San Quentin at this time as a pleasure resort where criminals out of sorts returned for a vacation.

I think their pictures of its attractions were overdrawn.

22.

ADMINISTRATION OF PRISON AFFAIRS UNDER THE LIEUTENANT-GOVERNOR RESULTED IN REVOLTS AND BREAKS AND FINALLY IN THE ESTABLISHING OF A BARBAROUS DISCIPLINE

When the State took charge of San Quentin Prison on October 11, 1860, I. N. Quinn, president of the Senate and Lieutenant-Governor, by reason of the succession of John G. Downey as Governor after the election of Milton S. Latham as United States Senator, automatically became Warden of San Quentin Prison. His term as Warden was brief, expiring on January 5, 1861, on which date the Senate elected Pablo de la Guerra its president, who became therefore *ipso facto* Lieutenant-Governor and Prison Warden. Governor Quinn, as we used to call him, however, remained at San Quentin as the representative of the large manufacturing interests. He was accidentally killed there three or four years later. His widow married Judge Alexander Campbell, one of the great criminal lawyers of that day. The only son of this later marriage has cut quite a figure in journalism, and is now managing editor of one of the big Los Angeles dailies.

The succession of Wardens under the old constitution may be interesting. All were lieutenant-governors directly elected by the people or elevated to the rank and emoluments of lieutenant-governor, as in the case of I. N. Quinn. They were: I. N. Quinn, Pablo de la Guerra, J. F. Chellis, T. N. Machin, William Holden, Romualdo Pacheco, William Irwin, and James A. Johnston. The latter was not connected by consanguinity or otherwise with the present Warden. By the constitution adopted in 1879, authority was vested in a board of directors of five members, with four-year terms.

One of the outstanding facts that must be recognized by any impartial investigation is that little or no improvement of conditions was attempted when the State took charge of San Quentin Prison. The peculiar but effective means of maintaining order and discipline employed by McCauley became by necessity obsolete. It would have been a hard stretch of official privilege for a warden to connive with convicts to facilitate their escape. Largely because of this, and because of the substitution of inferior officers and guards for McCauley's men of iron nerve, the prison was rocked with a long series of wholesale riots, revolutions, and breaks carried on with all the grimness of despair by the convicts, and repressed only at the cost of many lives.

More than once the entire convict body came within an ace of overpowering the guard and gaining their freedom. The most determined of these breaks took place on January 16, 1861, two weeks after Warden Quinn retired, and on July 22, 1862 and April 2, 1864. The last was the most spectacular, because the prisoners seized the person of Lieutenant-Governor T. N. Machin, ex-officio Warden, and hurried him along with them a distance of about two miles to what was then known as Ross Landing. The guards followed close, but the fugitives were in physical possession of the commanding officer, holding knives ground to a needle point to his neck, under which compulsion he ordered that his men not shoot.

Had they fired, no doubt remains that the prisoner would have cut Machin's throat at once. As the escaping men reached Ross Landing, they were set upon by an armed band of resolute farmers, woodchoppers, and men gathered together at the Landing. These rapidly organized an envelopment movement, which broke down the morale of the prisoners before the objective was reached—the heavily wooded flank of Tamalpais. This flight became a panic from which Machin was easily extricated. Many gave themselves up in despair. An effective fire was opened against those who still sought safety in the brush; a number were killed and others wounded, while some made their escape.

I have a very precise memory of that historic event. It was a beautiful April day when a horseman passed through the streets of San Rafael yelling like a madman that the convicts had broken out of San Quentin and were headed in a body for the county seat to rob the town and murder everybody. I have been through some interesting episodes in my life, but this particular one was surely a hummer. When the first panic subsided a bit, the small population prepared to sell life as dearly as possible. Most people gathered up their most treasured valuables and hurried to the adobe courthouse or the Marin Hotel, or the solitary store of Solomon Bear, which were deemed the best defensive quarters. There we waited, avid though resolute, but the escaped convicts never came our way. Doubtless because of these frequent breaks the prison discipline became cruelly harsh—beyond the border line of barbarity. Men were flogged inhumanly on the very suspicion of desire to escape. Some were confined in solitary cells on bread and water for weeks, months, and years. Some were given cells in the old dungeon, from which they emerged mere shells of men, as a rule physically ruined beyond all hope of repair. The "Water cure," which consisted of directing the stream of a high pressure fire hose against the prisoner's mouth and nose so as to shut off respiration to a great extent and produce an artificial strangulation, was particularly feared. Prisoners who would set their jaws and take twenty lashes on their backs, apparently unmoved, would break down completely before a water treatment. Other forms of punishment were employed with which I will not further harass the reader. But for twenty years under the State's administration it is perfectly safe to say than an average of ten prisoners went to the whipping post every day, not to mention solitary confinement, the dungeon, or the water cure.

As the prison was considered merely an appendix to politics, the personnel of the official family changed from Warden down to the humblest guard with every shifting wind of party supremacy. No one ever stayed on the job long enough to know much about it. Indeed, the main incentive was lacking, for whether a warden and his subordinates were good, or whether they were totally incompetent, the net results were precisely the same—all alike were thrown in the discard whenever a new administration came around. Therefore, as a purely casual employment, it behooved the incumbent to make hay while the sun shone. So far as any reform, any constructive attempt for the institution's betterment went, officials cared nothing whatever. All manner of illicit trade was conducted between convicts and guards. Opium and whisky were trafficked in for years. Monte and faro games were openly conducted in the yard whenever the patronage justified a play.

Several convicts, I have been told, who held the banker end of these games, were released with small-sized fortunes. Money was not "contraband." The prisoner was relieved of his cash and his valuables when he arrived. Thereafter it was up to him to recover a fresh supply from his relatives and friends, which was easy enough for the better fixed prisoners. Under such circumstances and conditions abuses were allowed to take deep, almost permanent root, some of which have not been entirely abated after the lapse of nearly sixty years.

The climate of Marin County is unusually healthful. The death record during most of the last period was remarkably low, especially in view of the fact that a large percentage of the prisoners received were already broken down by disease. But after the convicts were confined within a walled area, the place became little better than a pest hole. That was peculiarly true of tuberculosis. Prisoners were constantly being received far advanced in consumption, sometimes in the last stages of the disease. Knowing nothing of its contagious character or the myriads of bacilli contained in a minute particle of sputum, the authorities were not entirely blameworthy in permitting these unfortunates to sleep in the same cells with unaffected persons. The result was what might have been expected. Great numbers were carried off by this curse of humanity. To the Indians and half-breeds, a term in San Quentin was equivalent to a death-warrant.

23.

PREJUDICE OF THE PEOPLE AND PRESS AGAINST PRISONERS AND EX-CONVICTS IS ONLY GRADUALLY OVERCOME BY ACTION OF THE PAROLE LAW

Almost forty years elapsed before an experienced observer could detect with certainty something like a sun-up in San Quentin's hell. In this long darkness there may have been, now and then, a faint and far glimmer of light, but it was always a false dawn. After the State had been managing the institution for a quarter of a century, with no better success than the lessee, I became a member of the State Board of Prisons. One of the first facts that attracted my attention was that at least seventy-five percent of the prisoners wore neither underclothes nor socks; nothing, in fact, but the rather light uniforms and shoes furnished by the State. On bleak winter days it was a familiar spectacle to see numbers of them blue-lipped and shivering, huddled together lest animal heat escape. Just a little investigation showed that the hospital was crammed to its limits, that a multiude of sick, representing the hospital overflow, were laid up in their cells; that in consequence the manufacturing industries were perilously crippled by epidemics of bronchitis and influenza. That was some thirty years ago, and after so long a lapse of time I can hardly remember whether I sympathized with those frost-bitten prisoners or not. As like as not I did, for I have a fixed dislike of being cold myself. Anyhow, the condition seemed to me a losing game for the State, beyond doubt or preadventure.

But when I proposed to issue socks and underclothes for the prisoners, it was received with as much astonishment as if I had suggested giving them gold-headed canes. It was declared a gross, unpardonable waste of the money of the State. Nevertheless, the motion finally prevailed, when the purely economic features were more fully explained. Socks of rough but serviceable grade were bought and distributed. Sewing machines were purchased, and the women prisoners rapidly made warm and comfortable underwear of Canton flannel for their male companions in adversity. Results justified the financial wisdom of the experiment. The huge drug bill was cut in half. The receipts from the hire of convict labor to the manufacturers, on which the support of the prison to a large extent depended, increased during the winter weather by over 90 percent. It is hard to understand in the present day the bitterness of the public against any intelligent measure of prison reform. The whole attitude was one of uncompromising vengeance against criminals. The Goodwin Act, granting credits upon good conduct, roused the wrath of the State. An earnest protest was raised when the whipping post was abolished in 1880. Men who had given the subject of penology a painstaking study were denounced as maudlin sentimentalists and enemies of society. Prisoners were treated far too well was the all but universal comment. That San Quentin was a paradise for malefactors was a common belief.

To propose to the legislature an appropriation for the betterment of condition, such as new buildings to relieve the ghastly consequences of overcrowding, was to receive a prompt rebuke from the solons and draw on one's head a perfect avalanche of hostile criticism. It was only by a scientific demonstration, as in the case of the underwear and socks, that a particular change could pay, that one could find an entering place for the thin blade of the wedge.

The first forward-looking piece of legislation was raised in the session of 1893 by the enactment of a parole law. Before it was put into practical operation it was slightly amended at the session of 1895, when I was a member of the Assembly. Shortly after I was again appointed a member of the State Board of Prison Directors, serving a full term of ten years. Therefore, I was in at the birth and participated officially in the disheartening—at-times-almost-despairing—efforts to put this all-important measure on its feet. I call it "fundamental" advisedly, because it directed public attention for the first time to the fact that there really was hopeful human material confined behind the walls of our prisons. Prior thereto, "once a criminal, always a criminal" was regarded as an axiomatic statement, as self-evident and obvious as another axiom, that the shortest distance between two given points is a straight line. Nor was the public so ill-advised at that time. Cases of reformation were so few and far between as to have become practically negligible. How could it have been otherwise? The man who had experienced a jolt of several years in the degenerating atmosphere of San Quentin, even if he had the hope of leading a decent life, found it impossible. He emerged with a capital of five dollars, only to find himself a pariah against whom the avenues of respectable employment were closed—not to mention possible social intercourse with normal human beings. He was dogged by the officers of the law, and if by some chance he secured employment under an alias, his former record was inevitably revealed. Only here and there a resolute, capable swimmer kept his head against the adverse current. The vast majority were submerged in the underworld of crime.

The parole law was passed and approved before the public and the press understood its real purport. When both realized the meaning of its text, the law was forcefully denounced as a scheme for wholesale jail delivery. Under these circumstances, it behooved the directors to go exceedingly slow—to give the system the opportunity to be judged by ascertained facts. For that reason, mainly, paroles were granted sparingly, only to those whose crimes were of a minor degree of turpitude, and where the State seemed to be taking no chance at all. Even then a single blunder came near to ruining everything, and postponing for an indefinite period any real effort at reform.

Rather against the board's better judgment, we had paroled a couple of boys who had committed a long series of burglaries in Oakland. The parole was granted after an active propaganda was carried on in the best of faith by prominent ladies on both sides of the Bay. Both the boys went wrong. One was shot by a policeman while burglarizing a house in the city of Alameda. The other, the famous Majors kid, struck out for Utah, organized a band of desperadoes, terrorized an extensive section of that State, and killed two or three of the pursuing posse before being finally captured. The reader can imagine the uproar that these incidents raised throughout the state. They were "the type of murdering scoundrels the prison directors were turning loose to commit midnight robberies and take the lives of innocent people," shrieked the well-meaning editors from San Diego to Siskiyou.

The legislature of 1899 was about to convene, and nothing seemed more certain than the unconditional repeal of the parole law. Only the personal presence and influence of the directors saved the day. Outside of myself, the board was composed of exceptionally able and earnest men whose station in life guaranteed them a fair hearing. In spite of the lamentable Major's case, they knew that the parole law was essentially expedient and right. After a rather prolonged stay at Sacramento, the directors brought the new Governor, Henry T. Gage, to the same way of thinking. Thus the parole law was given another chance in life. Two years afterwards the directors were able to show a tabulated statement of results under the law that satisfied even the sharpest critic; and induced an entire change of attitude on the part of the press. At that time the law was applicable to first-termers only. Since then it has been widely and wisely extended.

Another thing I might mention here was the great difficulty experienced at first in securing proper employment for paroled men. Twenty-five years ago and later it was well-nigh impossible. The right people would have none of them. As a final outcome of the situation, paroled men were often entrusted to those who proved the worst exploiters, who worked the unfortunate men to death and beat them out of their wages, under threat of bringing about the forfeiture of their paroles. Such facts being demonstrated by investigation, the employment of paroled men was put on an organized basis, leading up to the highly efficient service of today.

Counting the two prisons, there are now not far from a thousand men at liberty under parole. At present prices it would probably cost the State a dollar per day per capita to feed, clothe, and guard them under confinement. By the end of the year this would amount up to some money. But that does not represent the most agreeable side of the picture, for nearly all these men are now engaged in productive industry, and therefore greatly adding to, instead of subtracting from, the wealth of the State. This applies to some extent as well to the large number of prisoners at present employed on State highway work.

The same board, at the legislative session of 1905, secured the first progress appropriation for building the new prison at San Quentin, which is the last link in the chain of evolution from the old prison hulk of James M. Estell.

24.

THE OLD ORDER THAT VIRTUALLY CONDEMNED A CONVICT TO A LIFE OF CRIME WAS GONE FOR GOOD UNDER THE ABLE AND HUMANE POLICY OF THE PRESENT WARDEN, WHO HAS ACCOMPLISHED MUCH GOOD

I have little more to add. The forward movement, once begun, has never ceased. The old order of things that virtually condemned a convict to a life of crime, thereby building up a huge permanent criminal class, has gone for good, to the everlasting advantage of the State. Under the able and humane administration of the present Warden, James A. Johnston, much has been accomplished in the way of practical work. With the new prison buildings completed, the inmates no longer suffer from overcrowding. They have ample food, and of the best; plenty of exercise, regular rest, careful regard for their health, together with the assurance that continued good conduct will earn a parole and another chance to make good in life. All this tends to material betterment in the present condition and future outlook of prison populations, and here an explanation is due. When I have used the word reform, it has been in a restricted sense. I did not intend to include it in a spiritual regeneration of the convict. That does not happen often, even among men who have never been in a prison at all. I consider a convict "reformed" when he has reached a point where he can be safely trusted at large, without danger of a further breach of the law, and whenever that point has been reached the State's duty to that man is at an end.

What I should consider a very valuable addition to what might be called the educational department of the prison is embraced in an excellent lecture course on purely practical subjects. "Back to the Soil" is one of the most popular slogans at the prison, and consequently most of the lectures deal with the cultivation of the soil and allied industries. I attended one of these lectures delivered by a U.C. instructor, a clever expert in his specialty of poultry raising. I was quite surprised to see a large roomful of attentive prisoners, notebook in hand, and still more perhaps, by their understanding of the subject matter, as clearly evident by the keen line of questions they shot at the speaker.

The organization of the health department, as it might be called, will not suffer by comparison with any institution, public or private, that I am familiar with. Tuberculosis has been cleaned up and the patients isolated in an open air ward on the top of the main cell building. Great attention is paid to the general subject of pathology, for often a close connection exists between some forms of disease and crime. The main effort is to return the prisoner to freedom in a much more resistant state of health than when he arrived. Dr. L. L. Stanley, Resident Physician of San Quentin, among other things, has developed thoroughly a simple cure for the opium habit, previously described in the columns of this paper, which has borne the acid test of experience by the late addicts after their release from prison. He adds also some of the devices of a beauty doctor. Often a man or woman has been sadly marked by nature to such an extent as to make their presence either forbidding or repulsive, hopelessly interfering alike with their happiness and progress through life. A harelip, a bad case of strabismus or "cock-eyes," or a ruined nose, plays perfect havoc with a man's chances and absolutely sours a woman's soul. Dr. Stanley has certainly worked wonders in the way of transforming these unfortunate facial derelicts into very presentable people. His "Before and After" group of photographs is one of the most interesting exhibits around the prison.

It was the universal belief among prison officers from the very beginning down to very recent times that in dealing with the more desperate class of criminals some measure of physical punishment, however regrettable it might be, was absolutely necessary to preserve even the semblance of discipline in the yard. It may be just as well to admit that I accepted this dogma myself. Nevertheless, corporal punishment has been outlawed for six or seven years, and without the expected catastrophe. Far lighter punishment, such as the loss of various privileges, like visits of friends, correspondence, and sometimes comparatively short periods of confinement in cells, seems to work as well as the whipping post, the straight-jacket, and the dungeon, which I always considered the worst of all.

All of which goes to prove to my way of thinking, that a policy of enlightened humanity is not only far more pleasant both for those who give and for those who receive, but is also a highly profitable investment. It is a matter of mathematical demonstration that the State of California is saving a sum running into millions a year through its changed attitude towards those who committed crime and paid the price. At the same time, unless my observations are wide of the mark, crime itself is on the wane, mainly, of course, because some of the main incentives thereto are in a fair way to be removed. Opium and its products are practically unobtainable by addicts, alcohol is on its last legs, dives, deadfalls, and the other houses of crime are being cleaned up. It is a long cry before our prisons, jails, and other like institutes of detention will bear upon rusty gates the legend "closed for want of inmates." But we are heading in the right direction, and in that direction I trust society will persevere.

I would respectfully suggest, in conclusion, a modification of the parole law as at present applied. The statute provides, in brief, that a prisoner may be paroled after serving one calendar year, or after serving seven calendar years of a life sentence. A parole is not a right, but an act of grace, and it is quite within the powers of the board of directors to withhold it indefinitely from an unworthy applicant. But a rule was passed by the board many years ago, requiring a prisoner to serve half his net term before he reached the eligible list. To be frank, I voted for that rule myself. At the time it was not strictly observed. Many were later paroled who were technically ineligible under this rule. Its real design was to silence public clamor against the parole law in its entirety.

The rule has subsequently become hard and fast. Yet I cannot but believe that there are many convicts in each prison who could be safely trusted at large who may not reach the eligible list for years. Prolonged confinement will not fit these men better in a final effort to make good. I think the time is singularly opportune either to relax the rule or revoke it altogether.

I cannot close this story without acknowledging my obligation to Frank C. Jordan for his ever generous help in necessary research work.

Also to Messrs. Morrison, Dunne & Brobeck for access to their extensive law library, and the premises in general I availed myself of their courtesy in so liberal a spirit that casual clients often mistook me for the head of the firm. Sometimes I fell into the same error myself.

In the large field of prison reform the *Bulletin* has taken an extremely active part and has made enemies in consequence; all of which was to be expected where public opinion is divided into hostile camps. Those who lead against archaic prejudices must be content to wait for posthumous vindication. As somewhat of an expert, I believe the services of this paper, in its hopeful effort to reconstruct the darkest element of humanity, will be recognized and remembered in the end.

II.

CONVICT NAMES, 1851-1854

Delivered to the State Prison up to November 23, 1854, *as far as they appear in office of State Controller.*

1851

December 8

Charles D. Brown, El Dorado Co.; John Brown, El Dorado Co.; Cyrus Williams, El Dorado Co.; George Williams, El Dorado Co.; Charles Currier, Sacramento Co.; George Galrun, Sacramento Co.; John Fisher, Sacramento Co.; Christopher Allen, Sacramento Co.; Owen Caruthers, Sacramento Co.; T. J. Hodges, Sacramento Co.; Joe Muriago, Sacramento Co.; Blucher Haskell, Sacramento Co. Nicholas Forbes, Sacramento Co.; William Galson, Sacramento Co.; Christopher Yacquer, Sacramento Co.; James Smith, Sacramento Co.; Juan Stephens, Sacramento Co.; Antonio Coria, Sacramento Co.

December 11

Patrick McManus; William Lear; Jos. Wilfred, all Tuolumne Co.

December 13

James Cochran; James Boland; Manuel S. Escaluta; Lewis García; José Valdez; Raymond García; George Franks, all San Joaquin Co.

December 15
James Wilson, Butte Co.; F. A. Campbell, Butte Co.; John Jackson, Mariposa Co.; Antonio Valensuelo, Mariposa Co.; José Selesar, Mariposa Co.; J. C. Arrigo, Mariposa Co.

December 16
Thomas Eagan; Wm. H. Perrier, both Placer Co.

December 23
John Rowland; Jame Davis [sic]; S. R. Stanley; R. A. Livingston; Manuel Aguerra, all Yuba Co.

1852

January 13
Henry Williams; David Dows, both Shasta Co.

February 14
Antonio Neverito, Colusa Co.

February 18
Lorenzo Amiezca; Benduren [sic]; F. Berry, all El Dorado Co.

February 20
Wm. Jones, Mariposa Co.

February 21
John Welsh; Wm. Dean, both Sacramento Co.

February 27
Yankee Jim (*alias* Jas. Robinson), San Joaquin Co.

March (date unknown)
John Paul; James Cadile, both Mariposa Co.

March 4
Wm. Edwards, Shasta Co.

March 15

Casimero Lara, Santa Clara Co.

March 23

Antonio Denietro, Tuolumne Co.

April 1

James Murphy, Placer Co.

April 11

Wm. Knight, San Luis Obispo Co.

April 13

Jothom W. Curtis, Sutter Co.

April 14

Marcellus Gay, Mariposa Co.

April 16

Manuel Silvear; Hugh B. Hethuty, both Tuolumne Co.

April 20

John Dougherty; Wm. Cunningham, both El Dorado Co.

May 6

Charles Guion; John Marvin, both San Joaquin Co.

May 7

Wm. Tabor; Edward Bugbee; Robert Dawson, all Sacramento Co.

June 12

Thomas Gillman, Placer Co.; James Bendall, Mariposa Co.

June 18

Marco Costelles, Calaveras Co.; John C. Carroll, Tuolumne Co.; Raymond Robalcalda, Tuolumne Co.

June 22
two state prisoners (unnamed), Trinity Co.

June 29
Thomas Brown; E. Rodríques; C. Ribera, all San Joaquin Co.

July 1
one convict (unnamed), Sacramento Co.

July 3
Manuel Gorse, Contra Costa Co.; Marco Soto, El Dorado Co.; Hiram Quimby, El Dorado Co.; John Francis, Calaveras Co.

July 8
Fleming Mopping; W. H. Hawkins; Agnes Reed; John Hawkins; Jos. Francis; Manuel Antonia, all San Francisco Co.

August 9
Y. Valenzuela, Mariposa Co.

August 14
James W. Clark, Calaveras Co.

August 18
Diego Flores, Solano Co.

August 20
Salidino Peraqueto; Gregino Sequeranda, all Tuolumne Co.

August 21
Chas. D. Farris, San Francisco Co.

August 25
Trinidad Pacheot, Tuolumne Co.

September 1

Jas. G. Loring; Wm. Harris, both San Diego Co.

September 4

Jos. Sweet; Carmeno Núñez; Gavier Gonzáles, all Sacramento Co.

September 20

Thos. Fuller, Napa Co.

September 23

John Wright, Butte Co.

September 29

Amenas McGarley; Richard Elliott; Joseph Kuhu, all San Francisco Co.

October 14

Geo. C. Bradley, Nevada Co.; Chas. Smith, Nevada Co.; Jas. Hoover, Nevada Co.; Juan Moran, Los Angeles Co.

October 15

José Gonzáles; Wm. Rives; Juan Pérez.; Dan Carlos; Robt. Smith, all Mariposa Co.

October 20

Pedro Ansa, Siskiyou Co.

October 22

Mateo Andrade, Monterey Co.

October 28

Geo. H. Swift, El Dorado Co.

November 8

Charles Alwin; Dolores Martínez; Lilly C. Smith; Henry Smith; Geo. H. Darrah, all San Francisco Co.

November 10
Wm. Taylor, Sierra Co.

November 13
Ternín Cruz; A. Hanson, both Tuolumne Co.

November 15
Rodiríquez [sic]; Thos. Durdan, both Santa Clara Co.

December 1
Pasquel Camillo, San Francisco Co.

December 4
John H. Green, San Francisco Co.

December 15
Jos. Sunderland; Antonio Fernando; Chas. N. Davis, all Calaveras Co.

December 21
Jas. Murphy, Placer Co.; John Wilson, Placer Co.; John W. Kelly, Placer Co.; P. Ramírez, San Francisco Co.

December 22
Peter Ord, Shasta Co.

December 25
Narcissa Gialeman; Jacob Williams, both San Joaquin Co.

December 29
Thos. Dowell, Trinity Co.

December 31
T. J. Jones; John Gordon, both Nevada Co.

1853

January 1

Pedro Gonzáles, Mariposa Co.; José María, Mariposa Co.; John Miller *alias* Dutchy, San Francisco Co.

January 15

Chas. T. Wingfield; W. H. Wingfield; Geo. C. Bridges, ; Francis Pérez, all Tuolumne Co.

January 17

Felicine Serrano; Henry Howard; Richard Smith; Wm. Morris, all San Francisco Co.

February 7

Henry Pitt, San Francisco Co.

February 14

Román Rangel, Monterey Co.

February 23

José Quivález, Mariposa Co.; Alexander Miclon, San Joaquin Co.; J. C. Swinbith, San Joaquin Co.; Alex. Vanderstraburg, San Joaquin Co.; Martínez Rodríquez, San Joaquin Co.; Mañana Gregblin, San Joaquin Co.

March 4

Wm. Hunger; Ahing [sic]; Amoi [sic], all El Dorado Co.

March 7

Juan Ruiz; Francisco Vera; John Campbell, all San Francisco Co.

March 9

Lewis Goddiot; John Bartley; Isaac Lery; John Brood; Thos. Henry, all San Francisco Co.

March 18

John Williams; John G. Elversan, both Sacramento Co.

April [date unknown]

Jesús Raeno; David B. Pierson, both Santa Clara Co.

April 11

Saml. Hall, Shasta Co.

April 14

Geo. W. Hice, Calaveras Co.; Robt. Pattern, Placer Co.; John Twitchler, Placer Co.; Wm. Smith, Placer Co.; F. P. Monson, Placer Co.; Wm. Moresen, Placer Co.; Chapman Bethell, Placer Co.

April 16

Juan [sic]; Henry King, both Los Angeles Co.

April 18

Richard Watkins; Wm. Davis; José Sepúlvera; Richard Murphey; Wm. V. Evens; Wm. Powers, all San Joaquin Co.

April 19

John Sullivan, San Francisco Co.

April 26

Wm. G. Comstock, Sonoma Co.

May 5

Pasquel Carrillo, San Luis Obispo Co.

May 10

Andrew Austin; Danl. Sales, both Santa Clara Co.

May 16

Henry Jansen, Nevada Co.

May 18

Abner Bishop; Raymond Palachio; Aboy [sic]; Stewart Butler; Alum [sic], all San Francisco Co.

May 25

A. H. Herbert, El Dorado Co.

June 9

José García, Contra Costa Co.

June 15

Wm. White; Wm. Fleck, both Placer Co.

June 17

John Arrington, Trinity Co.

June 19

John Cahill, Calaveras Co.; Jean B. Michael, Calaveras Co.; Wm. Thompson, Calaveras Co.; Lester Imperial, Calaveras Co.; Saml. McClintic, Calaveras Co.; Dennis Orton, Siskiyou Co.

June 20

Marian Wilson; Wm. Sanders; Thos. O'Neal; José Palajo, all San Francisco Co.

June 23

M. F. White; Wm. Turner, both San Joaquin Co.

July 11

Jesús Pecardillo, Mariposa Co.; Fernern Báldez, Los Angeles Co.

July 13

John Sebastian, Calaveras Co.

July 27

Wm. Thompson; Feliciano Guarro; John Legg, all San Francisco Co.

August 2

G. F. Hendry, Sacramento Co.; John Branden, Sacramento Co.; Wm. Carter, Sacramento Co.; E. H. Conner, San Joaquin Co.; Jas. Atkins, San Joaquin Co.; H. A. Stevens, San Joaquin Co.; W. J. Henry, San Joaquin Co.

August 6

Alex. Freeman; Clinton Taylor *alias* C. L. Taylor, both San Francisco Co.

August 8

Wm. Hartley, Placer Co.; Victor Contrearción, San Francisco Co.; Peter Mahan, San Francisco Co.

August 11

James Ervin; J. D. Loring; Jas. Luck; Saml. Cohen; Wm. Williams; Y. Valensuelo, all Mariposa Co.

August 12

Rafel Galenti, Monterey Co.

August 17

Hiram Durham, Calaveras Co.

August 18

Thos. Brown, Siskiyou Co.; John Maguin, San Francisco Co.

August 19

Geo. Wright; Wm. Powers; Jack Bowen; P. Montagu, all San Francisco Co.

August 30

Saml. Lago, Tulare Co.

August 31

Emanuel Cheviarias; Jas. Hodden; L. E. Cushman, all Sacramento Co.

October 1
Chas. Crane, Sacramento Co.

October 10
Antonio Gonzáles; Lewis Frank, both Mariposa Co.

October 15
Montague Lyons, Sierra Co.

October 17
Salzero [sic], Calaveras Co.

October 19
Ni Yai; Danl. McMillan, both San Joaquin Co.

October 29
Chas. Ley, Placer Co.

October 31
Juan García; David Duncan; Francis Medina; Jas. Pool; Manuel Parrara; James Wallman; Jesús Santo, all Tuolumne Co.

November 7
Jas. McNulty; Jas. Camanche, both Sacramento Co.

November 8
1 convict [unnamed], El Dorado Co.

November 14
Geo. Riley, Sacramento Co.

November 19
Ignacio Roono; Jack Fairow; Geo. M. Fairrow, all Yuba Co.

December 2
Jesse Bennett, El Dorado Co.

December 7

John Anderson, Sacramento Co.

December 22

Wang You Fou, Calaveras Co.

December 27

Domingo [sic], Santa Barbara Co.

December 29

John Knipley, Monterey Co.

1854

January 3

Timothy Donovan; Thos. Ashton; John Gustavus, all El Dorado Co.

January 4

John H. Harper; Henry Garthoff, both Butte Co.

February 6

Pablo Massey; Roland Hughes; John Schmidt, all El Dorado Co.

February 19

Robt. Warren, Calaveras Co.; D. W. Duncan, Calaveras Co.; Wm. Ogley, San Joaquin Co.; John J. Ogley, San Joaquin Co.

February 28

Jas. V. Gates, Sacramento Co.

March 8

John R. Hammond; Edmund Coy; John Wright; Thos. Fielding, all Yuba Co.

March 9

José A. Rodríquez, Los Angeles Co.; Whitman Valentine, Tuolumne Co.; José Rylas, Tuolumne Co.; John Mondih, Tuolumne Co.

March 22

Jim Cony, Sacramento Co.; Wm. Peters, Sacramento Co.; Thos. Mitchell, Sacramento Co.; Joshua N. Giddings, Sacramento Co.; 5 convicts (unnamed), Mariposa Co.

April 4

Peter Nicholas, Tuolumne Co.

April 10

Manacia Moreno, Los Angeles Co.; Wm. Brown, Monterey Co.; 1 convict (unnamed), Solano Co.

April 13

Frank Wilcox, Yuba Co.; John Caldwell, Mariposa Co.; Thos. Mancello, Mariposa Co.

April 15

Jesús [sic], Mariposa Co.

May 7

John Brown; Philip Arnest; Peter Barton; John Burger; Geo. Humphries, all Sacramento Co.

May 17

J. R. Weldon; Isan [sic]; Henry F. Lauran; J. R. Guthrie, all El Dorado Co.

May 24

Horace Brewster; John Carey, both Placer Co.

May 25

Pedro Madria; Francis Padell; Mark Israel; Jacinto Zañiga; Sebastín Buteria; Pedro Riez, all Contra Costa Co.

May 29
John Henderson, *alias* Boyle, Sierra Co.

June 3
John Conner; Francisco Abarro, both Siskiyou Co.

June 12
J. A. Marshal, Yuba Co.; Cyrus Peters, Yuba Co.; Andrew Rombo, Contra Costa Co.

June 19
N. E. Johnson; John Johnson, both Butte Co.

June 21
Edward Campbell; John Robinson, both San Joaquin Co.

June 22
Damasio Pérez; C. Monico, both Calaveras Co.

June 24
J. C. Barelas, Los Angeles Co.

July 6
Raphail Martínez; L. Ballarto, both Yuba Co.

August 4
Juan Chapo, Los Angeles Co.

August 11
Henry M. Knox, San Joaquin Co.; Sacramento Valenzuelo, Contra Costa Co.

August 14
Henry Dobbar, Solano Co.

August 15
Wm. LeCount, El Dorado Co.; John G. Aldrich, El Dorado Co.; John W. Potts, El Dorado Co.; Cullin Douglas, El

Dorado Co.; Wm. Hurlbert, El Dorado Co.; Henry Harper, Tuolumne Co.; Francis Brown, Tuolumne Co.

August 17

Pasquel Guergo; María Gonzáles, both Mariposa Co.

August 20

Chas. Cardon, Yolo Co.

August 21

Jos. Malcomson; Jacob Kinsey, both Yuba Co.

August 25

Wm. McCam; Wm. Courtney; Peter Miller; Jas. Low, all Calaveras Co.

August 31

Ah Wah, Sacramento Co.

September 9

Jas. Goodine, Butte Co.

September 14

A. Edwards, Placer Co.

September 24

John Dean; John Gallager; Clark Curry, all Siskiyou Co.

October 2

John Porter; C. G. Smith; Henry A. Stephens; Jas. R. Atkins, all Sacramento Co.

October 5

Jas. Newland, Solano Co.

October 14

Lude Fernaspen, Tuolumne Co.

October 18

Robt. D. Wilmot, Yuba Co.; Wm. Bryant, Yuba Co.; A You, Yuba Co.; John Auch, Sierra Co.

October 20

Geo. Sullivan, Nevada Co.

October 22

Wm. Harrington; Geo. Williams; Michael Hunt; John Savage, all San Francisco Co.

October 27

We Sing, Placer Co.

October 28

John Smith, Sacramento Co.

October 29

Henry Hensley; M. Campbell; Wm. Hall; Geo. Taylor, all San Francisco Co.

November 3

B. C. Smith, Trinity Co.

November 7

Geo. Dashwood; Saml. Barker; Alex. Williams, all San Francisco Co.

November 8

James Graham; David Hermathy; John McClelland; James Minturn; Ervin Payne; Chas. Stevans; P. Davidson; S. T. Cochran, all Sacramento Co.

November 22

Manuel Valdineso; Chas. Massenger; John Andrew; Henry Smith, all San Francisco Co.

III.

SAN QUENTIN: AN ANNOTATED BIBLIOGRAPHY

BY BONNIE L. PETRY

Aronoff, B. R. *Dead Man Walking: A Matter of Time*. Red Bluff, CA: Eagle Pub., 1991, 305 p., glossary, introduction by Ken Harris, California Department of Corrections.
Ben Aronoff, a musician, takes a job teaching San Quentin inmates to play guitar in 1982, and over the next three-and-a-half years, goes from guitar teacher to prison guard to hobby manager before he is dismissed. "I began an unbelievable journey into the 'nonworld' world of prison, incarceration, and the California Department of Corrections—a journey that took me to the scum capital of the universe and, I think, back again"—Prologue. "While reading this book you will learn of the politics and corruption that prevail in California corrections. Some of what you read may be hard to believe. I can attest that Ben's portrayal is quite accurate"—Introduction.

Barrie, John. *Inside San Quentin Today*. San Quentin, CA: Esque Distributors, 1965, 47 p., 24 black and white photographs.
In 1961 John Barrie was appointed Supervisor of Recreation at San Quentin. In this booklet, he attempts "...to play the role of guide and interpreter, and to present a simple, objective picture of life inside San Quentin"—Introduction. He focuses on the facility itself, the basic process each inmate goes through from admittance to release, and their educational, vocational, and recreational opportunities.

Barry, John Daniel. *Hanging at San Quentin Prison.* San Francisco, CA: Monadnock Pub. Co., 1912, 11 p.

Blevens, Carl. *In the Hills and Hollers.* San Quentin, CA: Month of Mondays Press, c1987.

Bonner, John C. *Hang Tough.* Minneapolis, MN: Bethany Fellowship, 1968, 122 p.
"A brief examination of the problems of penology with special emphasis upon the pathological personality; namely, the 'philosophies' of San Quentin inmates."

Braly, Malcolm. *False Starts: A Memoir of San Quentin and Other Prisons.* Boston, MA: Little, Brown, 1976, 375 p.
The autobiography of a man who describes himself as "...a liar, a sneak, a braggart, a show-off, and a thief"—p. 4. Malcolm Braly was in and out of jail for much of his life before finally finding success as a writer. The book received good reviews. *The New York Times* said "...this illuminating book is not merely an honest look at a life of crime but, rather, an honest look at a life, period."

Braly, Malcolm. *Felony Tank.* Greenwich, CT: Fawcett Gold Medal Books, 1961, 175 p., paper.
This novel "...established him as a singularly informed, objective, and truthful writer of criminal fiction...," says Anthony Boucher, writing for the *New York Times.*

Braly, Malcolm. *It's Cold Out There.* New York: Pocket Books, 1976 (c1966), 192 p., paper.
Braly's third novel "...is especially notable for its creation of a dangerously neurotic charmer and for its depiction, more vivid that I know elsewhere in fiction, of the reactions of the paroled convict to the harsh, cold outside world."—Anthony, Boucher writing for the *New York Times.*

Braly, Malcolm. *The Master.* New York: Warner, 1973, 158 p., paper.

"Based on an original screenplay by Alan Trustman and Harry Kleiner."

Braly, Malcolm. *On the Yard: A Novel.* Boston, MA: Little, Brown, 1967, 344 p.

Says Kenneth Lamott, writing for *Book World*, "This is virtually the only convincing novel of prison life I have read..." Kurt Vonnegut proclaimed it "...the great American prison novel."

Braly, Malcolm. *The Protector.* New York: Jove Books, 1979, 189 p., paper.

Based on a screenplay by Richard Levinson and William Link, this novel depicts the plight of the inhabitants of an apartment building on the bad side of town who hire an over-zealous private guard to protect them.

Braly, Malcolm. *Shake Him Till He Rattles.* Greenwich, CT: Fawcett Gold Medal Books, 1963, 175 p., paper.

Brown, Christopher. *Leo's Fifth Expression.* San Quentin, CA: Month of Mondays, c1987, 14 p.

Poetry. "A product of the Arts-In-Corrections Program of the California Department of Corrections."

Brown, Michael D. *The History of Chino Prison: The First Fifty Years of the California Institution for Men, 1941 to 1991.* Chino, CA: Vocational Offset Printing Program, California Institution for Men, Chino, 1991, 199 p.

Written to commemorate California Institute for Men's golden anniversary on June 21, 1991. Includes a brief history of San Quentin's early years on p. 1-25.

Carlshausen, H. Buderus von. *America!—Add Stars to Our Stripes*, by "Roark Tamerlane" [pseud.], #59071. San Quentin, CA: [no publisher], c1943, 87 p.

Chattman, Elmo. *Beads of Wax.* San Quentin, CA: Month of Mondays Press, San Quentin State Prison, 1987, 15 p.

Poems. "Product of the Arts-in-Corrections program of the California Department of Corrections."

Chessman, Caryl. *Cell 2455: Death Row.* New expanded edition. Englewood Cliffs, NJ: Prentice-Hall, Inc., 1960, 402 p.

Caryl Whittier Chessman, convicted of seventeen counts of robbery, sex perversion, and attempted rape, was given the death sentence and sent to San Quentin in 1948. It was not the first time he had been there. He successfully postponed his execution eight times before finally going to the gas chamber on May 3, 1960. While reviewers disagreed somewhat on the quality of the writing, they all said that Caryl Chessman's autobiography was important for the insights it provides into a criminal's mind, if nothing else. It quickly became a best seller. The expanded edition contains an extra chapter prepared by Chessman's literary agent from material contained in his two other books, *Trial by Ordeal* and *The Face of Justice*, and from unpublished sources.

Cleaver, Eldridge. *Soul on Ice.* New York: McGraw-Hill, 1968, 210 p., introduction by Maxwell Geismar

Leroy Eldridge Cleaver was in and out of prison from age twelve. In 1957-1958 he was charged with assault to commit rape and assault to commit murder, convicted and sent to San Quentin, where he stayed until 1963, when he was transfered first to Folsom, then to Soledad. Cleaver became a key figure in the Black Muslim movement. Gertrude Samuels, writing for the *Saturday Review*, said that Cleaver "...has produced an original and disturbing report on what a black man, reacting to a society he detests, reacting to life behind bars for nine years, finally becomes."

Collins, William. *Black Bart: The True Story of the West's Most Famous Stagecoach Robber.* Mendocino, CA: Pacific Transcriptions, 1992, 272 p.

Charles Boles, also known as Black Bart, "...is the best known and most prolific stagecoach robber in American history and has become a legend in California and the

West"—Preface. He was caught and sent to San Quentin on November 21, 1883, where he became prisoner #11,046. He was released on January 21, 1888. This profusely illustrated, highly readable, and meticulously researched book is the first book devoted solely to Black Bart's history. Seven appendices offer interesting supplemental material, such as the full text of the bogus *San Francisco Examiner* interview with Black Bart.

Cummins, Eric. *The Rise and Fall of California's Radical Prison Movement.* Stanford, CA: Stanford University Press, 1994, 319 p.
"This is a first-rate work by a participant in the radical California prison movement of the late 1960s and early '70s."—K. Edgerton, writing for *Choice*.

Davidson, R. Theodore. *Chicano Prisoners: The Key to San Quentin.* New York: Holt, Rinehart and Winston, 1974, 196 p., foreword by George and Louise Spindler. Series: Case studies in cultural anthropology.
"My fieldwork among prisoners at San Quentin began in June 1966, when I was a graduate student at the University of California, Berkeley. Prison administrators wanted to see if an anthropologist could determine what subcultural factors were responsible for Mexican-American prisoners being excessively violent and excessively reluctant to participate in rehabilitation activities."—Introduction. Davidson takes a holistic approach to understanding the Chicano prisoner culture and does not pull any punches. List of chapters: The Setting, Entry into the Prison World, The Reality behind the Formal Prison Life Cycle, Types of Prisoners, Baby Mafia or Family, Prisoner Economy, Sociopolitical Prison Leadership, Social Control, Conclusion.

Davis, Bernice Freeman. *The Desperate and the Damned.* New York: Thomas Y. Crowell, 1961, 229 p.
Bernice Freeman Davis was the San Quentin correspondent for the *San Francisco Chronicle* for eighteen years. "An absorbing series of tense yet factual reports written with taste

and restraint..."—P. G. Anderson, writing for *Library Journal*.

Day, Robert. *Seppuku Sunset.* San Quentin, CA: Month of Mondays Press, San Quentin State Prison, 1987, 15 p.
Poems. Product of the Arts-in-Corrections program of the California Department of Corrections.

Douglass, Royall. *Prison Verse*, by Royall Douglass, no. "19173," San Quentin. Palo Alto, CA: Altruria Press, 1911, 32 p., foreword by Donald Lowrie.
A beautifully produced booklet printed on thick paper with a decorative gold border on each page. The cover has an ink drawing of a stone wall with an iron gate. A photograph of San Quentin is set into the wall. Below this appears the title Drops of Blood, and below that, the musical notation for the song "Taps," with the rounded parts of the notes rendered in red. The foreword is by Royall Douglass's former cellmate. Nineteen poems entitled: Stained, Release, The Open Road, A Christmas Sonnet, At a Numbered Grave, Sonnets of the Hours, The Garden of Death, A Nocturne, Love's Warder, The Death Watch, A Roman Holiday, Shadows, Sunset, Absence, Rose of Seville, The Land of Dreams, The Call, Blind Eros, Sepulture.

Duffy, Clinton T., with Al Hirshberg. *88 Men and 2 Women.* Garden City, NY: Doubleday & Co., 1962, 258 p.
Born August 4, 1898 to a San Quentin guard, Clinton T. Duffy grew up at San Quentin, ultimately becoming Warden there in 1940. He was responsible for many reforms and was, ironically, against capital punishment. The title refers to the total number of executions Duffy supervised during his eleven-and-a-half years as Warden of San Quentin. Said the *New York Times*: "This book is a seemingly endless parade of the unfortunates who passed through Death Row on their way to the execution chamber."

Duffy, Clinton T., with Eva Irene Linkletter. *From Heroin to San Quentin.* Morro Bay, CA: Java Books, 1977, 304 p., introduction by Eva Irene Linkletter, preface by Clinton T. Duffy, "Narcotic Quotes" by Senator Alan Cranston.

A novel depicting the downward spiral of a fictional heroin addict and his eventual return to society. Details are drawn from "...many cases I was familiar with over my thirty-two years with the California Department of Corrections..."—Preface.

Duffy, Clinton T., as told to Dean Jennings. *The San Quentin Story.* Garden City, NY: Doubleday & Co., 1950, 253 p.

Duffy's autobiography of his San Quentin years. This book received good reviews and was the inspiration for two motion pictures.

Duffy, Clinton T, with Al Hirshberg. *Sex and Crime.* Garden City, NY: Doubleday & Co., 1965, 203 p.

Duffy theorizes that sex is the cause of most criminal behavior and attempts to support this by relating appropriate case histories. This book "...adds nothing to the literature except to give the instructor in criminology another horrible example of unscholarly writing"—J. J. Baldi, writing for *Best Sellers.*

Duffy, Gladys Carpenter, with Blaise Whitehead Lane. *Warden's Wife.* New York: Appleton-Century-Crofts, 1959, 346 p.

Gladys Carpenter, the daughter of a San Quentin guard, was the childhood sweetheart of Clinton T. Duffy. Her autobiographical book was well-received. *Kirkus Reviews* proclaimed it "...a thorough documentary of life in prison and living among prisoners that instructs while it reveals." Frank O'Leary, writing for the *Saturday Review*, noted her no-nonsense approach, saying, "...this is one of the richest treasuries of prison and underworld anecdotes and vignettes this reviewer has read in a lifetime of interest in the subject."

Durden-Smith, Jo. *Who Killed George Jackson? Fantasies, Paranoia, and the Revolution.* New York: Alfred A. Knopf, 1976, 292 p.
This book received mixed reviews. Phillippa Merriman, writing for *Library Journal*, said the "...author's confusing account of Jackson's death and his research into it emerges as a vehicle for what the book is really about: Durden-Smith's own disenchantment with the New Left and its esposal of Jackson."

From Soledad to San Quentin. San Francisco, CA: Prison Solidarity Committee, 1970, 27 p.

The House at San Quentin: Proposals for Expansion. Berkeley, CA: University of California, Graduate Studio 200B, 1986, 35 p.
"This booklet describes four design schemes of varying sizes developed for The House at San Quentin. The House, operated by the Catholic Social Services of Marin, offers childcare, hot meals, clothing loans, and hospitality to people visiting inmates at San Quentin Prison. It has a small, paid staff and many volunteers who help on a part-time basis. Services may soon be expanded to include counseling for visitors and a 24-hour infomation hot line"—Introduction. Four remodeling plans illustrated with renderings and photographs of scale models.

Howard, Clark. *American Saturday.* New York: Richard Marek Publishers, 1981, 319 p.
Called "controversial" by two different reviewers, this is a novelized but not fictionalized account of the events that took place between 12 A.M. and 3 P.M. on Saturday, August 21, 1971 at San Quentin, the day George Jackson was killed during an attempted escape. By coincidence, while doing research for another book, Clark Howard learned that George Jackson had grown up in the exact same Chicago neighborhood he did; in fact, they were only a block away from each other. "Why then, I wondered, did George Jackson end up face-down on the San Quentin yard with a

gun guard's bullet in him, while I was now a moderately successful writer of books? Was it only because of the color difference? I could not quite swallow that. In some ways Jackson had a lot better chance to make it than I did. He was black, but he had two parents, food on the table, decent clothes, and was getting a good education in the relative calm of a Catholic classroom. I, although white, had no parents (a junkie is not really a parent), was always hungry, wore threadbare clothes, and attended one of the toughest public schools in the city. Jackson had one other thing, too, that I do not remember. He was loved"—Author's note. Intrigued, Clark Howard decided to learn everything he could about George Jackson; this book is the result.

Howard, Harry, Chaplain, as told to Chaplain Ray. *Changed Lives in San Quentin.* Dallas, TX: Acclaimed Books, 1986, 202 p., foreword by Daniel B. Vasquez, Warden, San Quentin Prison, introduction by Max Call.

The stories of eight convicts and how religion changed their lives. The last chapter is a brief biography of Harry Howard, who began his duties as Protestant chaplain at San Quentin in 1974. The last four pages of the book appear to reproduce the text of a pamphlet promoting religion which is circulated at San Quentin.

Howland, Larry O. *San Quentin and Beyond.* Monroeville, PA: Whitaker House, 1974, 192 p. Foreword by Wesley E. Smith.

Son of a dysfunctional family with an abusive father, Larry O. Howland drifts into a life of crime. Convicted of murder, he is sent to San Quentin and eventually gets religion, the main focus of this autobiography.

In His Own Shoes. San Quentin, CA: San Quentin State Prison, c1986, 47 p.

Anthology of poems "...written by members of the Literary and Poetry Workshop at San Quentin State Prison." "A product of the Arts-in-Corrections program of the California Department of Corrections."

Jackson, George. *Soledad Brother: The Prison Letters of George Jackson.* New edition. New York: Bantam Books, 1972, 248 p., paper, introduction by Jean Genet.

In 1959, at the age of eighteen, George Jackson was sentenced from one year to life for stealing $70 from a gas station. The next eleven years of his life were spent in prison. In 1968 he was charged with the murder of a Soledad guard. In 1970 he was transfered to San Quentin, where he was shot and killed during an escape attempt on August 21, 1971. This new edition contains material previously unpublished, and was completly revised by Jackson before his death. *Library Journal* said, "Jackson presents evidence of the degradation of black existence unexplored by the Kerner Commission and other federal investigating bodies."

Jackson, Spoon. *No Distance Between Two Points.* San Quentin, CA: Month of Mondays Press, San Quentin State Prison, 1987, 15 p.

"Product of the Arts-in-Corrections program of the California Department of Corrections."

Johnston, James A. *The Prison Problem and What Is Being Done to Solve It at San Quentin: An Address by James A. Johnston Delivered Before the Stockton and San Joaquin County Teachers' Institution: At Stockton, California, November 27, 1916.* San Francisco, CA: J. H. Barry Co., 1916, 14 p.

Lamott, Kenneth Church. *Chronicles of San Quentin: The Biography of a Prison.* New York: David McKay Co., 1961, 278 p.

A very detailed and well-researched history of San Quentin from August 1849, when the city government of San Francisco purchased the stranded hulk of the sailing ship, *Euphemia*, to serve as a city prison, to 1960.

Lamson, David Albert. *We Who Are About to Die: Prison as Seen by a Condemned Man.* New York: Charles Scribner's Sons, 1935, 338 p.

In 1933 David Lamson was tried and convicted of the first degree murder of his wife and sentenced to death by hanging. Thirteen months later the California Supreme Court overturned the verdict, and he was released from San Quentin. Richard Elman, writing for *The Georgia Review*, refered to this book as "...a memoir of simplicity and originality about his time on death row which remains one of the strongest first-person prison books I have ever read." The full text of the California Supreme Court Decision that reversed the order of the trial court is appended to the book.

Leibert, Julius Amos, with Emily Kingsbery. *Behind Bars: What a Chaplain Saw in Alcatraz, Folsom, and San Quentin.* Garden City, NY: Doubleday & Co., 1965, 223 p.

Rabbi Leibert, who served as chaplain in Alcatraz, Folsom, and San Quentin, finds that prisons do not stop crime. Arcadi Nebolsine, writing for *Commonweal*, noted that "...to criticize the faults and the (perhaps unavoidable) superficialities of the work is not to say it should not be read. There is enough nobility in it and enough of fact to give it great value and any attempt to remind the reader of the injustices of prison life is of value. The Rabbi knows what he is talking about."

Lewis, Roy V. *The Squires of San Quentin: An Evaluation of a Juvenile Awareness Program.* Sacramento, CA: Dept. of the Youth Authority, 1981, 162 p. Series: Crime and juvenile delinquency: 1981 update; no. JD 662.

"This report presents an evaluation of the San Quentin Squires Program. Operated in California since 1964, it is the oldest juvenile awareness program in the United States."—Introduction. "...Our research findings indicate that a moderately confrontive youth awareness program such as Squires has some beneficial effects on less delinquent youth but no effect on more serious delinquents."—Conclusions.

Lewis, Roy V. *The Squires of San Quentin: Executive Summary*. Sacramento, CA: Dept. of the Youth Authority, 1981, 5 p.

Lewis, Roy V. *The Squires of San Quentin: Preliminary Findings on an Experimental Study of Juvenile Visitation at San Quentin Prison.* Sacramento, CA: Dept. of the Youth Authority, Division of Research, 1979, 136 p. Series: Crime and juvenile delinquency: 1980 update; no. JD 628.

London, Jack. *The Star Rover.* New York: Macmillan Co., 1915, 329 p.
Based on the experiences of Ed Morrell, convict #14486, who began his life of crime in 1891, and gradually became one of the most notorious convicts at San Quentin. He claimed that he was able to use something he called "mind projection" to leave the confines of San Quentin and wander in spirit form. Thanks to Warden Major John W. Tompkins, who took an interest in him, Morrell became head trusty of San Quentin and eventually had his life sentence commuted in 1908.

Lowrie, Donald. *Donald Lowrie's Story: Back in Prison Again—Why?: New and Amazing Serial in the* Call *Describes One Man's Long, But Losing Battle for Freedom.* San Francisco, CA: 1925, 30 p. At head of title: *The San Francisco Call and Post.* Originally published serially; reprinted in one volume.

Lowrie, Donald. *My Life in Prison.* New York: Mitchell Kennerley, 1912, 422 p.
Without food or a home for three days and prospects of more of the same despite his best efforts, Donald Lowrie flipped his last nickel to decide whether he should commit suicide or burglary. Burglary won. He was sentenced to fifteen years in San Quentin, where he arrived on July 24, 1901 and became #19,093.

Lowrie, Donald. *My Life Out of Prison.* New York: Mitchell Kennerley, 1915, 345 p.

Lynch, Jack. *San Quentin: A Bragg Novel.* New York: Warner Books, 1984, 267 p., paper.

McKanna, Clare V. "Ethnics and San Quentin Prison Registers: A Comment on Methodology," in *Journal of Social History* 18:3 (Spring, 1985): 477-482.
"In recent years social historians have provided statistical analyses offering new perspectives on how police, prosecutors, judges, and juries have handled criminals. Only a handful of these studies have focused on prison inmates. Prison registers offer researchers a readily available source of data that tell a good deal about prison inmates and also may reveal bias and prejudice within the criminal justice system. But few researchers have taken the time to explore or evaluate the usefulness of these sources..."—beginning of article. An analysis of the data recorded at San Quentin from 1851-1880.

Mann, Eric. *Comrade George.* Cambridge, MA: Hovey Street Press, 1972, 64 p.
"Comrade George, an investigation into the official story of his assassination. His work for the people and their response to his death. Red Prison Movement."

Marshall, Bertha. "Librarian Goes to San Quentin," in *California Library Bulletin* 11:3 (March, 1950): 101-102.
A brief article about Herman K. Spector, Senior Librarian in charge of the library at San Quentin, and his library.

Minton, Robert J., ed. *Inside: Prison American Style.* New York: Vintage Books, 1972, 325 p., paper.
A collection of writings from California convicts, including the full text of *A Convict Report on the Major Grievances of the Prison Population with Suggested Solutions from San Quentin.* Shane Stevens, writing for the *New York Times Book Review*, said "In harrowing detail [this book] documents the brutality, injustice, corruption, and deadly hypocrisy of a system that murders men's minds as it destroys their bodies."

Moore, J(oseph) Wess. *Echoes from the Tomb of the Living Dead.* Berkeley, CA: Keystone Publishing, 1908, 16 p. Life convict No. 18,759, California State Prison at San Quentin.

Morrell, Ed. *The Twenty-Fifth Man: The Strange Story of Ed Morrell, the Hero of Jack London's Star Rover*, by Ed Morrell, Lone Survivor of the Famous Band of California Feud Outlaws. Montclair, NJ: New Era Publishing Co., 1924, 390 p. Foreword by George W. P. Hunt, Governor of Arizona, introduction by Dr. Raymond S. Ward.
Ed Morrell's autobiography. "The contribution of Ed Morrell to society in calling attention to the cruel, inhuman and utterly indefensible prison system, is a service that only men like him are competent of rendering."—Foreword.

Norvell, Smokey. *For Lavetta.* San Quentin, CA: Month of Mondays Press, San Quentin State Prison, 1987, 14 p.
"Product of the Arts-in-Corrections Program of the California Department of Corrections."

Owen, Barbara A. *The Reproduction of Social Control: A Study of Prison Workers at San Quentin.* New York: Praeger, 1988, 160 p.
Michael Benson, writing for *Choice*, called this book "A rare investigation of the role of prison workers as seen from the worker's perspective. In a clear, readable style, Owen describes the social world of prison workers..." Robert C. Hauhart, writing for *Journal of Criminal Justice*, noted that the "...study also suffers from precisely the feature which distinguishes it: it is a study of prison guards that relies on their own accounts and understandings as the primary source of evidence. While this permits Owen intimately to reconstruct the guards' worldview, it does not permit her to measure the guards' worldview against some other objective reality."

Pettaway, James. *C-44137*. San Quentin, CA: Month of Mondays Press, San Quentin State Prison, 1987, 15 p.
Poems. "A product of the Arts-in-Corrections program of the California Department of Corrections."

Presley, Robert B. "Marin County and San Quentin Show the Way: Combined Jail/Prison Siting Offers Advantages," in *California County* (March-April, 1990): 10-11.
"Siting, building, and operating joint jail/prison facilities with the state is one way for counties to cut costs and keep up with the need to construct new jails." Senator Robert B. Presley relates the search by Marin County for a replacement site for the Silveira Ranch honor farm, whose lease expired in 1992, and discusses the advantages.

Randall, Belle. *San Quentin and Two Kinds of Conscience*. Berkeley, CA: 1961.
This poem won first prize in the Emily Chamberlain Cook Prize in Poetry competition.

San Quentin Days: Poems of a Prison. Sacramento, CA: Press of J. M. Anderson, c1905, 31 p.
A collection of nineteen poems by an anonymous author: Destiny, Reconciliation, Retrospect, Memory, Youth, To Billy, Agnosticism, Violets, Longing, Challenge, Sleep, A Sonnet to -, Justice, Mirage, Return, A Letter, Some Day, A Pipe, and Paroled. The cover art depicts a scene of the sun setting across a bay and a prison wall encircled by a ball and chain. There are sepia-tone line drawings throughout.

San Quentin Minstrel and Vaudeville Company. San Quentin, CA: The Company, July 4, 1911, 10 p.

"San Quentin—The Effects of a Court Order," in *FCL Newsletter* (Friends Committee on Legislation of California) 34:5 (May 1985): 1 p.
"In September 1983, California Superior Court Judge Beverly Savitt held in *Wilson v. Deukmejian* that San Quentin main-line prisoners were being confined under

conditions which violated both the California and United States Constitutions. A year later the governor signed a bill appropriating $21,860,000 for repairs mandated by the court order." This article briefly discusses the improvements made thus far, and the work that then remained.

Schneider, Wilma. *Woman on the Gun Wall.* Millbrae, CA: Les Femmes Pub., 1978.

Spector, Herman K. *Juvenile Delinquency: A Bibliography.* San Quentin, CA: 1963, 109 p.
Herman K. Spector was the senior librarian who ran the library at San Quentin from 1947-68. Recruited by Warden Clinton T. Duffy, Spector had been a librarian at the Penitentiary of the City of New York and chief librarian of the New York Dept. of Corrections. "His library became renowned as possibly the best prison library in the land, partially owing perhaps to Clinton Duffy's public relations success."—Eric Cummins, *The Rise and Fall of California's Radical Prison Movement*, p. 21. All inmate writings that left San Quentin were subject to censorship. While other employees censored the mail, Spector was responsible for censoring and confiscating, if necessary, everything else. This selective bibliography lists 643 items relating to juvenile delinquency.

Spector, Herman K. *The Library Program of the California State Department of Corrections.* Sacramento, CA: s.n., 1956, 24 p.

Spector, Herman K. *What Men Write in Prison.* [S.l. : s.n., 1958?], 7 p.
Reprinted from *Tomorrow* 5:4: 53-56.

Stanley, Leo Leonidas, with the collaboration of Evelyn Wells. *Men at Their Worst.* New York: D. Appleton-Century Co., 1940, 332 p.
Dr. Leo Leonidas Stanley was Chief Surgeon of San Quentin for 38 years, from 1913-51. This autobiographical book of

his San Quentin experience, written after he had been there 27 years, received mixed reviews, most favorable. Despite the title, one chapter, "The Women," is devoted to the female convicts at San Quentin. In the chapter, "Why I Believe in Sterilization," he argues for sterilization of certain types of prisoners. Another chapter, "Sex and Crime," details the great lengths the guards went to in order to prevent homosexual activity among the prisoners. Stanley also describes his experimentation with glandular rejuvenation, an attempt to rejuvenate old men by transplanting bits of other men's testicles into them.

Stanley, Leo Leonidas. *My Most Unforgettable Convicts.* Winnipeg, Manitoba: Greywood, 1967, 137 p., foreword by Walter C. Alvarez, M.D.
A collection of anecdotes about various convicts all of whom the author met with the exception of Black Bart, the famous stagecoach robber. The beginning chapter relates how he survived the first physical attack of his San Quentin career, although he was outnumbered three to one. Some of the anecdotes are merely brief rewritings of excerpts from *Men at Their Worst.*

Stanley, Leo Leonidas. *Tuberculosis in San Quentin.* San Francisco, CA: 1939 (1938), 15 p. Reprinted from *California and Western Medicine* 49:6 (December, 1938), and (January, 1939).
When Dr. Stanley assumed his duties at San Quentin, he found a high incidence of tuberculosis among the inmates, which he was able to bring under control.

Stanley, Leo Leonidas. *Twenty Years at San Quentin.* [n.p.]: 1938, 15 p. Excerpt from *The Centaur of Alpha Kappa Kappa* 39:2 (January, 1934).
Another collection of anecdotes from the so-called "Chief Croaker."

Steinbeck, John. "The Hanging at San Quentin," in *Avon Short Story Monthly: 10 Great Stories: A New Anthology.* New York: Avon, 1945, p. 11-22.
This is chapter nine from Steinbeck's novel, *Pastures of Heaven.* Raymond Banks, now a successful poultry farmer, was the high school friend of Ed who became Warden of San Quentin. Whenever there's a hanging, Ed invites Ray.

Tannenbaum, Judith. *The Real Rap: A Message to the Youth.* San Quentin, CA: Month of Mondays Press, San Quentin State Prison, c1989, 80 p.

Tasker, Robert Joyce. *Grimhaven.* New York, London: Alfred A. Knopf, 1928, 241 p.
Robert Joyce Tasker was sentenced to five years to life for robbery and sent to San Quentin Prison. "Since Robert Lowrie years ago wrote *My Life in Prison* and popularized thereby the cause of prison reform, nothing from a convict's typewriter has approached the sheer force and competence of *Grimhaven.*"—*World Tomorrow.*

Taylor, Jay C., "Poppa Smurff." *Face in the Mirror.* San Quentin, CA: Month of Mondays Press, San Quentin State Prison, 1987, 15 p.
Poems. "This is a product of the Arts-In-Correction Program of the California Department of Corrections."

University of California. School of Criminology. *The San Quentin Prison College Project: Final Report, Phase I.* Berkeley, CA: University of California. School of Criminology, 1968, 79 p.

Walker, Buck D. *A Convict Report on the Major Grievances of the Prison Population, with Suggested Solutions.* Sacramento, CA: 1969, 84 p.
Presented to the Assembly Committee on Criminal Procedure at San Quentin, February 18, 1969. The full text of this report may be found in *Inside Prison American Style*, edited by Robert J. Minton, Jr. Twelve items: Refixing the

Term of Imprisonment, Parole Violations, Long Terms Served by Parole Violators, Adding Crimes, First-Time Offenders, Time Served, Others' Crimes, The Voice of the Public, Changing Policies, Records, Changing Expectations, and The Media. Nine appendices: Certification of Adult Authority Action, Conditions of Parole, Parole Violation Charges, Parole Report, Transcripts of Adult Authority Hearings, Decisions to Release or Not to Release, Crime and Penalties in California, The Sense of Injustice, and AB 581: What Rights for Convicts?

Zastrow, Jane. "Working Next to the Chain Gang: San Quentin Remodeling Project Places Special Burdens on Construction Manager and General Contractor," in *Northern California Real Estate Journal* 3:13 (March 27-April 9, 1989): 13-16.

PERIODICALS

American Indian Cultural Group Newsletter. San Quentin, CA: San Quentin Prison, Vol. 1, no. 1 (Dec. 1968)- .

The Outlaw.
An underground newspaper illegally published by San Quentin inmates for 14 months from June 1967 to August 1968. The primary focus was investigation of prison rumors. "The staff went to great efforts to stop *The Outlaw*. Soon after the convict paper began publication, every duplicating machine in the prison was under lock and key; but it continued to be published, and a copy of each issue appeared on the warden's desk!"—R. Theodore Davidson, *Chicano Prisoners: the Key to San Quentin*, p. 185.

San Quentin Bulletin.
"...an occasional literary magazine which began publication in 1925."—Kenneth Lamott, *Chronicles of San Quentin*, p. 204. Discontinued by Warden Court Smith in 1937. Richard

Joyce Tasker and Richard Krebs (pseudonym Jan Valtin) were the most notable contributors that went on to become well-known authors.

The Index.
"...the earliest known San Quentin publication was a semi-monthly magazine called *The Index*, published in John Hoyle's administration. Although printed by hectograph, it was well written and attractive."—*Chronicles of San Quentin*, p. 204.

The News. San Quentin, CA: California State Prison at San Quentin, 1941-1946, 6 v. Weekly. Vol. 1 (Jan. 7, 1941)-v. 6, no. 19 (July 5, 1946).
"The other side of the inside." Continued by *The San Quentin News*.

The San Quentin News. Tamal, CA: San Quentin, 1946- , biweekly. Other title: *San Quentin News Bulletin*, Oct. 3, 1986. Vol. numbering inconsistent: part of vol. 7 called vol. 5; vol. 8 repeated in numbering. Continues: *The News* (California State Prison at San Quentin).

San Quentin Sports-News. San Quentin, CA: California State Prison at San Quentin. Library of Congress has incomplete microfilm set from v. 2, no. 26, October 2, 1934 to v.8, no. 20, December 24, 1940. Also called the *Green Sheet*. Continued by *The News*.

Wall City News. Continued by *San Quentin Sports-News*.

GOVERNMENT DOCUMENTS

California. *Documents Connected with the State Prison.* Senate. Doc.; no. 7. sess. 1853. George Kerr, State Printer, Sacramento: 1853, 26 p.

California. Attorney General's Office. *Opinion of the Attorney General in Response to Senate Resolution, Adopted February 16, 1866, Relating to the Tide Land Locations upon the San Francisco City Front, near Oakland, and the State Prison.* San Francisco, CA: O. M. Clayes, State Printer, 1866, 8 p.

The Senate resolution John G. McCullough, Attorney-General responded to reads: "Resolved, That the Attorney-General be requested to communicate to the Senate all material facts within his knowledge concerning provisions for and sales of tide lands within the five mile limits of the Cities of San Francisco and Oakland, and one mile of the State Prison at Point San Quentin, together with his opinion as to the validity of such sales."

California. Dept. of Corrections. *Business Administration and Industries in State Correctional Service.* San Quentin, CA: State of California, Department of Corrections, 1959, 130 p. Series: Correctional employees training manual: 7.

California. Dept. of Corrections. *California Department of Corrections Plan to Implement the Findings of the Court, Wilson vs. Deukmejian: Phase I Report, San Quentin State Prison.* Sacramento: The Dept., 1983, 111 p.

California. Dept. of Corrections. *Correctional Employees Training Manual A: Orientation to Employment in State Correctional Service.* 3rd edition. Sacramento, CA: California Dept. of Corrections, 1950-1955, 6 v. in 1.

CONTENTS: 1. California Institution for Men, Chino, 1951. 2. California Medical Facility, Terminal Island, San Pedro,

1952. 3. California State Prison at Folsom, 1950. 4. California State Prison at San Quentin, 1950. 5. California State Prison at Soledad, 1950. 6. Deuel Vocational Institution, Tracy, 1955. Foreword to volume four by Richard A. McGee, Director of Corrections. Preface by Clinton T. Duffy, Warden.

Table of contents for volume four: Part I—Orientation to the California State Prison at San Quentin: Chapter 1—Purpose and Scope of Orientation Training, Chapter 2—Conditions of Employment, Chapter 3—Institutional Organization and Program, Chapter 4—Institutional Procedures, Rules and Regulations. Part II—The Employee's Approach to Training: Chapter 5—How to Study Effectively, Chapter 6—How to Improve Your Reading. Appendix A—Check Sheet For the New Employee. There is a photograph of the prison, a sample of a blank performance report for probationary employees, an organizational chart, and a map of the prison.

California. Dept. of Corrections. *Final Plan to Implement the Findings of the Court: Wilson vs. Deukmejian: Phase II report.* Sacramento: The Dept., 1984, 132 p.
"On September 13, 1983, a Declaratory Judgment and Permanent Injunction was issued by the Superior Court of the State of California for the County of Marin, in the case of Wilson vs. Deukmejian. In this case, the Court decreed that inmates comprising the mainline population at San Quentin State Prison suffered cruel and unusual punishment and were denied due process of law....the text of this report contains the plans of the Department to eliminate, ameliorate, and correct each condition cited by the Court as unconstitutional."—Introduction. Overcrowding, the inmate classification system, operational and structural deficiencies are the problems addressed by this report.

California. Dept. of Corrections. *Introduction to State Correctional Service.* 3rd edition. San Quentin, CA: State of California, Department of Corrections, 1962, 104

p. Series: Correctional employees training manual; 1. Prepared by R. R. Rollins and R. K. Procunier.

California. Dept. of Corrections. *Orientation to Employment in State Correctional Service: Correctional Employees Training Manual A.* Sacramento, CA: California State Prison at San Quentin, 1950, 35 p.

California. Dept. of Corrections. *Plan to Implement the Findings of the Court: Wilson vs. Deukmejian.* Sacramento, CA: The Dept., 1983, 2 v.

California. Dept. of Corrections. *Biennial Report / Dept. of Corrections.* Title varies: *Progress Report*, 1944, 1967/68. Title varies: *Correctional Progress in California*, 1961/62-1965/66. Title varies: *Status Report*, 1972-1974. Sacramento, 1944-[1972-1974]. First report covers the period from May 1 to Nov. 30, 1944.

Includes reports of the Adult Authority; Board of Trustees of the Institution for Women; State Board of Prison Directors; State Prison, San Quentin; State Prison, Folsom; Institution for Men, Chino and Institution for Women, Tehachapi; California Vocational Institution; Medium Custody Prison at Soledad. Bound in 2 v. Continued by: California. Dept. of Corrections. California Department of Corrections: [report]. Ceased publication 1968? Report year ends Nov. 30.

California. Dept. of Finance. Financial and Performance Accountability. *Department of Corrections, California State Prison at San Quentin, Inmate Welfare Fund: Examination of Financial Statements for the Period [July 1, 1974 to June 30, 1993*]. Sacramento, CA: Financial and Performance Accountability, Dept. of Finance, State of California, 1977-1994, 12 v.

California. Dept. of Finance. Fiscal Management Audits. *California State Prison at San Quentin, Improvements to Various Physical Facilities: United States Department of Commerce, Economic Development Administration,*

Examination of Grant no. 07-51-21775 for the Period September 16, 1977 to May 4, 1979. Sacramento, CA: Fiscal Management Audits, Dept. of Finance, State of California, 1979, 10 p.

California. Dept. of Finance. Organization and Cost Control Division. *Management Survey for the Department of Corrections: Cash Trust Records & Procedure, San Quentin Prison.* Sacramento, CA: s.n., Oct. 11, 1957, 3 p.

California. Dept. of Public Health. Bureau of Food and Drug Inspections. *A Survey of Food Purchase, Preparation and Serving at San Quentin Prison.* Berkeley, CA: s.n., 1939, 1 vol., various pagings.

California. Governor (1931-1934: Rolph). *In re Case of Jack D. Green, San Quentin no. 51811, Application for Executive Clemency.* Sacramento, CA: 1934, 12 p.

California. Governor's Investigation Committee on Penal Affairs. *Final Report.* Sacramento, CA: s.n., January 21, 1944, 56 p. Appendix to Senate Journal, 55th session, 3rd extra session 1944.

"On November 29, 1943, Governor Earl Warren appointed a committee to investigate the penal and correctional institutions of the State. The Governor requested the members of the committee to make a thorough and unbiased investigation of all State penal institutions and the correctional schools, and to submit a written report setting forth the facts found by the committee."—Introduction. "The history of prison management in California reveals scandal after scandal and a sordid record of mismanagement. Many previous studies have been made....all coming to the same conclusion that the whole administrative structure needs to be reorganized. The report of your special investigating committee is, in fact, merely a current confirmation of the facts and recommendations made many times in the past by other investigating groups."—Letter of Transmittal to

Governor Warren. This report, examining the overall picture, occupies the first section of this document (to p. 22). Separate reports on individual institutions appear as appendices on p. 23-56. The San Quentin report (p. 27-32) examines housing capacity, general administration, prisoner involvement in preparation of confidential records, religious services, escapes, discipline of inmates, classification of inmates, employment of inmates, accounting, education, the prisoner's merit system, degeneracy (homosexuality), and inmate authority, among other topics.

California. Governor's Investigation Committee on Penal Affairs. *Preliminary Reports of Governor's Committee on Penal Affairs: Folsom Prison: San Quentin Escapes on December 26, 1943.* Submitted to Honorable Earl Warren, Governor of California. December 14, 1943 and Dec. 31, 1943. Sacramento, CA: California State Printing Office, 1944, 39 p. Appendix to *Senate Journal*, 55th session, 3rd extra session, 1944.

California. Governor's Investigation Committee on Penal Affairs. *Proceedings of the California Governor's Investigating Committee on Penal Affairs, 1943 Dec. 4 - 1944 Jan. 18.* Description: 14 v. in 3 boxes (1.25 linear ft.)

Transcript of proceedings: v.1-5, Folsom Prison; v. 6-7, San Quentin; v.8, Whittier State School for Boys; v.9, Ventura School for Girls; v.10, San Quentin; v.11, California Institute for Women at Tehachapi; v.12, California Institute for Men at Chino; v.13, Preston School of Industry; v.14, Operations of the Bureau of Paroles and the Board of Prison Terms and Paroles.

California. Joint Committee of the Senate and Assembly. *Report on the State Prison by the Joint Committee of the Senate and Assembly, 1873-1874.* Sacramento: G. H. Springer, State Printer, 1874, 91 p.

California. Legislature. *Reports of Standing and Select Committees of Senate and Assembly of California Relative to the Condition and Management of State Prisons: Record of the Proceedings of the Senate and Assembly Relative to the Same Matter.* California: s.n., 1903, 24 p.

"On cruel and unusual punishments, especially straight-jackets." Witnesses testified that convicts had been crippled and sometimes killed by punishment with the straightjacket. The Warden, Martin Aquirre, and other San Quentin officials denied everything. Two of the committee members ventured to try it for themselves, and claimed no harmful effects, but the committee as a whole was divided on the topic.

California. Legislature. Assembly. Committee on Prisons and Reformatories. *In the Matter of an Investigation Respecting Punishment and the Use of the Strait Jacket at the State Prisons at Folsom and San Quentin, by a Subcommittee of the Committee on Prisons and Reformatories of the Assembly: Hearing: San Quentin, March 26, 1913.* Sacramento, CA: s.n., 1913, various pages.

California. Legislature. Assembly. Select Committee on Prisons and Reformatories. *Report...on Conditions at the State Prisons at San Quentin and Folsom.* Sacramento, CA: s.n., 1913, 19 p. Excerpt from *Assembly Journal*, Appendix 22, 1913.

California. Legislature. Assembly. Special Committee on State Prison Reform. *Report.* Sacramento, CA: s.n., 1907, 16 p.

California. Legislature. Joint Committee of the Senate and Assembly. *Report on the State Prison by Joint Committee of Senate & Assembly.* Sacramento, CA: State Printer, 1856, 36 p.

California. Legislature. Joint Commmittee on Prison Construction and Operations. *San Quentin Prison: Current Problems and Possible Solutions: Hearing by Joint Committee on Prison Construction and Operation.* Sacramento, CA: The Committee, 1983, 113 p. "September 27, 1983, In-Service Training Center, San Quentin Prison, 10 A.M.-12:30 P.M. Senator Robert Presley, Chairman." Cover title: *California's Prisons: San Quentin: First of a Series of Hearings Held by the Joint Legislative Committee on Prison Construction and Operations.*

On April 24, 1983, San Quentin Prisoners brought a class-action suit before Judge Savitt of the Marin County Superior Court, claiming that living conditions in the older sections were so bad that inprisonment in San Quentin was unconstitutional. Judge Savitt visited the prison twice—once unannounced—and discovered such things as a dead rat in the bakery, overcrowding, a substandard electrical system, and deteriorated plumbing. This is the transcript of a hearing prefaced by a one-page history of San Quentin, newspaper articles from the *Los Angeles Times* and the *New York Times*, a summary of the conditions discovered by Judge Savitt, and other documents.

California. Legislature. Senate. *Report of Special Committee Appointed to Ascertain the Amount of Controller's Warrants Issued During the Year 1855, on Ac't of State Prison.* Sacramento, CA: State Printer, 1856, 35 p.

California. Legislature. Senate. *Speech on Senate Floor, May 22, 1957: Concerning Death Penalty by Senator Fred Farr.* Sacramento, CA: s.n., 7 p.

California. Legislature. Senate. *Visit by Senator Fred Farr to San Quentin Death Row, May 10, 1957.* Sacramento, CA: s.n., 7 p.

California. Legislature. Senate. Rules Committee. *Hearing [August 8, 1994]* / Senate Rules Committee, State of California; reported by Evelyn J. Mizak. Sacramento, CA: Senate Publications, 1994, 111 leaves. "State Capitol, room 112, Sacramento, California." "Monday, August 8, 1994, 2:32 P.M." Senate Publications stock no.: 260-R.

California. Legislature. Senate. Special Committee to Investigate State-Prison. *Report of the Senate Investigating Committee, Relative to Affairs at the State-Prison.* Sacramento, CA: J. O. Meara, State Printer, 1859, 121 p.

California. Legislature. Senate. State Prison Committee. *Report of Committee Relative to the Condition and Management of the State Prison.* Sacramento, CA: B. B. Redding, State Printer, 1855, 70 p. Senate. Doc. no. 25, Sess. 1855.

California. Office of the Attorney General. *Opinion of the Attorney-General in Response to Senate Resolution: Adopted February 16, 1866, Relating to the Tide Land Locations upon the San Francisco City Front, Near Oakland and the State Prison.* San Francisco, CA: O. M. Clayes, State Printer, 1866, 8 p.

California. Office of the Attorney General. *Report of the Attorney-General Concerning the Title to State Prison Lands at Point San Quentin: In Accordance with the Joint Resolution of the Two Houses.* Sacramento, CA: Benj. P. Avery, State Printer, 1863, 20 p.

California. State Board of Prison Directors. *Report of the State Board of Prison Directors of the State of California.* Sacramento, CA: The Board, 1880-1931, 32 v. Biennial. Included are reports of the state prisons at San Quentin and at Folsom. Report year ends June 30. Report for 1896/98 never published. Continues: California. State Prison Direc-tors. Report.

California State Board of Prison Directors. *Rules and Regulations for the Government of Prisoners, California State Prison at San Quentin.* San Quentin, CA: San Quentin Press, n.d., 22 p. Cover title. "A few words from the warden," p. 4-7.

California. State Joint Committee on Defectives. *Surveys in Mental Deviation in Prisons, Public Schools and Orphanages in California, Under Auspices of the State Joint Committee: Brief Description of Local Conditions and Need for Custodial Care and Training, Dependent, Defective, and Delinquent Classes.* Sacramento, CA: State Printing Office, 1918, 87 p. At head of title: California State Board of Charities and Corrections.
CONTENTS: Report of the State joint committee; A partial psychological survey of the prison population of San Quentin, California, based on mental tests of 155 consecutive entrants, by L. M. Terman and H. E. Knollin; Backward and feeble-minded children in the public schools of "X" County, California, by L. M. Terman, V. Dickson and L. Howard; The intelligence of orphan children and unwed mothers in California charitable institutions, by J. H. William; The mental examination of 75 children at the "Y" home, by Grace M. Fernald.

California State Prison at San Quentin. *California State Prison at San Quentin and Other Locations: Lists of Officers, Employees and Prisoners, 1856-1858.* Pomona, CA: Pomona Valley Genealogical Society, 1991, 3 p.

California State Prison at San Quentin. *California State Prison at San Quentin Records, 1851-1910.* 1 portfolio.
Includes releases, 1852, by James M. Estell for John C. Hays and John Caperton from contracts with the prison; agreement between Estell and J. F. McCauley, 1857; letter from an

inmate, notice of escaped prisoner; accounts, and other materials. From the W. Scott Polland Collection.

California State Prison at San Quentin. *California State Prison at San Quentin Records, 1885-1952.* 7 v.
Includes letterpress copybooks for 1885 and 1908; index register; county register, ca. 1950-52; description of prisoners, 3 v. Also with these: record book of prisoners discharged, 1903-10 (prison not identified).

California State Prison at San Quentin. *Descriptive Registers of Prisoners, 1851 Jan. 25-1940 Jan. 20.* 17 vols.

California State Prison at San Quentin. *Duties of Officers, Guards and Employees and General Rules: October 1st, 1928: California State Prison at San Quentin, California.* San Quentin, CA: San Quentin Press, 1928, 11 p. Signed: Jas. B. Holohan, Warden.

California State Prison at San Quentin. *The Great Decisions Program.* [Sacramento?: s.n.], 1960.

California State Prison at San Quentin. *The Libs Meeting, October 14, 1960.* San Quentin, CA: 1960, 10 p.

California State Prison at San Quentin. *Illegal Forfeiture of Credits: A Convict Must Be Found Guilty of a Distinct Violation of a Rule, Legal Forms Must Be Followed by the Prison Directors, Action of the Directors Can Be Reviewed.* [Sacramento?: s.n., 1890?], 4 p.

California State Prison at San Quentin. *Lethal Gas Chamber, San Quentin State Prison.* San Quentin, CA: The Prison, 1992, 30 p. Cover title. "Issue date: 10/18/84; revised date: 4/92."

California State Prison, at San Quentin. *List of Convicts on Register of State Prison at San Quentin, Marin*

County, CA: Alphabetically Arranged—Complete, August 31, 1889. Sacramento, CA: State Office, J. D. Young, Supt. State Printing, 1889, 404 p.
"Immediately and rigidly suppressed by the state. John McComb was removed from his position of Warden as a result of the publication of this book."—note laid in.

California State Prison at San Quentin. *New Year Vaudeville, San Quentin, California, New Year's Day, 1923: Show Produced and Presented by Harry Ettling.* San Quentin, CA: San Quentin Press, 1923, 12 p. "Souvenir Programme, New Year Vaudeville, San Quentin, Cal., 1923, New Year's Day."
Under Warden John Hoyle, who took office in 1907, many reforms were instituted, including holiday shows organized by the prisoners. The New Year's Day show became more elaborate over the years until it finally occupied the entire day. For example, the show for 1913 "...started off with a grand minstrel show, folowed by olio acts, 'German' comedians, Spanish dancers, an artistic club swinger, a female singer, buck-and-wing dancers, a close-harmony quartet, several skits, a comic monologue, a 'Laughable Afterpeice,' and movies of the Flynn-Johnson fight."—Kenneth Lamott, *Chronicles of San Quentin*, p. 184.

California State Prison at San Quentin. *New Year's Jamboree*. San Quentin, CA: n.d.

California State Prison at San Quentin. *Outline of Condition of Employees, California State Prison—San Quentin*. San Quentin, CA: n.p., 1954, 3 p.

California State Prison at San Quentin. *Report of the Educational, Library and Religious Activities for the Biennium Ending June 30, 1928*. S.l.: s.n., 1928, 13 p.

California State Prison at San Quentin. *Report of the Lessee of State Prison, to the Legislature of the State of California, February 14, 1855*. Sacramento, CA: B. B.

Redding, State Printer, 1855, 6 p. Series: [Legislature] 1855. Senate. Doc. 12

Report presented Jan. 28, 1855, by J. M. Estell, lessee, for the superintendent of the prison. Prefixed to the "Annual Report of Inspectors of State prison [for 1854] (Senate doc. 13, 1855)"

California State Prison at San Quentin. *Prison Record Book, for San Quentin and Folsom Prisons, 1904-1911.* 2 boxes.

Originally one volume (26 cm x 41 cm), now boxed in two parts: Box 1: Portraits; Box 2: Data Sheets. Data sheets, including photographs, of prisoners being discharged.

California State Prison at San Quentin. *Sentences Imposed and Time Served in Prison in Several Penal Institutions in the United States.* [Sacramento?: s.n., 1936], 13 leaves.

California State Prison at San Quentin. *Table of General Statistics of San Quentin Prison from January 25th 1851 to January 31st 1903.* 1 p.

California State Prison at San Quentin. Dept. of Education. *The Department of Education, State Prison, San Quentin, Marin County, California: A Survey of General Functions and Activities Prepared Under the Supervision of Harry Andrew Shuder, Director.* S.l.: s.n., 1936.

California State Prison at San Quentin. Furniture Dept. *School, Institution and Office furniture.* San Quentin, CA: San Quentin Press, 1936, 66 p.

California State Prison at San Quentin. Furniture Dept. *School, Institution and Office Furniture, Flags, Tinware: Manufactured at California State Prison at San Quentin.* San Quentin, CA: San Quentin Press, 1930, 29 p.

California State Prison at San Quentin. Library. *Employees Library, California State Prison, San Quentin, California: A Joint Project of the Library and in Service Training Units*. S.l.: s.n., 1950, 10 p.
A list of publications held by the library.

California State Prison at San Quentin. Library. *Exhibit of Special Books, California Library Week, March 6-12, 1955*. San Quentin, CA: s.n., 1955, 6 p.

California State Prison at San Quentin. Library. *I Read Because...: A Group of Essays Written by Our Inmate Library Users*. San Quentin, CA: n.p., 1964, 40 p.
Herman Spector ran an intensive bibliotherapy program during his years at San Quentin. This collection of essays may reflect the prisoners' estimations of what Spector wanted them to read.

California State Prison at San Quentin. Library. *The Library*. S.l.: s.n., 1949. On cover: With compliments of the Special Libraries Association.

California State Prison at San Quentin. Library. *A List of Books, Journals, and Pamphlets Which Cover the General Fields of Criminology and Penology*. San Quentin, CA: 1956, 16 p.

California State Prison at San Quentin. Library. *Men and Books, Books and Men*. San Quentin, CA: 1960, 20 p. Cover title: *Books and Reading*.

California State Prison at San Quentin. Library. *The Prison Library of San Quentin: Its Program and Its Achievements*. S.l.: s.n., 1949, 15 p.

California State Prison at San Quentin. Library. *Welcome, American Library Association, Annual Conference, July 13-19, 1958*. [S.l.: s.n., 1958?], 5 p.

California. State Prison Directors. *Report.* Sacramento, CA: 185?-1899.

Included are reports of the State Prison at San Quentin. Continued by the reports of the State Board of Prison Directors, constituted by law of 1880. A report for 1856 was never published.

California. Superior Court (Marin County). *Don C. Wilson; Richard Parento; and Ursula Gealey, Plaintiffs, vs. George Deukmejian, Governor of the State of California; M. A. Chaderjian, Secretary of the Youth and Adult Corrections Agency of the State of California; Daniel McCarthy, Acting Interim Director of the California Department of Corrections; and Reginald Pulley, Warden of San Quentin State Prison, Defendants: No. 103454, Tentative Decision and Proposed Statement of Decision.* S.l.: Superior Court of the State of California in and for the County of Marin, 1983, 27 p.

On April 24, 1983, San Quentin Prisoners brought a class-action suit before Judge Savitt of the Marin County Superior Court claiming that living conditions in the older sections were so bad that inprisonment in San Quentin was unconstitutional.

CRS Sirrine. *Executive Summary: San Quentin State Prison, Tamal, California.* San Francisco, CA: CRS Sirrine, 1986, 13 p. Cover title: Executive summary: long range plan, value engineering study, cost benefit analysis. Summary of *Long Range Plan...*, listed below.

CRS Sirrine. *Long Range Plan: Long Range Plan Value Engineering Study Cost Benefit Analysis: Cost Benefit Analysis: San Quentin State Prison, Tamal, California.* San Francisco, CA: CRS Sirrine, 1986, 1 v. (various pagings). Prepared in cooperation with the California Dept. of Corrections.

Jaman, Dorothy R. *Characteristics of Violent Prisoners, (San Quentin—1960): Research Report, California.* Dept.

of Corrections, no. 22. Sacramento, CA: California Dept. of Corrections, 1966, 31 p.
"The California Department of Corrections' Research Division is engaged in a study to attempt to predict violence within its institutions, as well as violence in the community by its parolees. As a first step of this major study, there was undertaken a descriptive study of the inmate who commits violence."—p. 1. Out of fifty-five variables tested, ten had statistical significance.

Snowden, Richard N. *Reply to Report of the Joint Legislative Committee on State Prison, by the State Board of Directors, with a Portion of the Suppressed Testimony.* Sacramento: California State Documents, v. 1, no. 12., 1856, 13 p.

Task Force on the Keldgord Report and San Quentin. *Report to Marin County Board of Supervisors on Implementation of The Keldgord Report in Marin County Submitted by Task Force on the Keldgord Report and San Quentin.* San Raphael, CA: The Task Force, 1973, 89 p. Cover title: Prison Task Force report to the Marin County Board of Supervisors.
The Keldgord Report is the common name for the statewide California Correctional System Study requested by Governor Reagan which was released to the public in July 1971. Conclusions of this study: while California's penal system has a reputation for being progressive, this actually occurs on a limited basis in isolated places; furthermore, the penal system is not a single system, but a collection of 121 separate agencies with no coordination among them, and "...the only place where the rehabilitative process was currently being carried out with any measure of success is within the community." As part of the recommendations of the Keldgord Report that rehabilitation take place at the county level, the Task Force "...concurs in plans to close San Quentin and recommends that the Marin County Board of Supervisors begin immediately to plan for a community

corrections system." A major portion of the report is devoted to examining alternatives to ordinary prisons.

THESES

Apostolos, Robert James. *The Effects of Prison Population Trends at San Quentin on Prison Reform Legislation in California: An Historical Study in Strategies of Control, 1850-1920.* San Diego, CA: San Diego State University, 1977, 207 p.
Thesis (M.S.)—San Diego State University, 1977.

Banks, Hobart Melvin. *An Analysis of Violence in San Quentin Prison.* Davis, CA: University of California, Davis, 1983 (c1982), 102 p.
Thesis (Ph.D.)—University of California, Davis, 1982.

Beseman, Harold. *A Historical Survey: Punishment and Prison Education.* San Francisco, CA: San Francisco State College, 1951, 76 p.
Thesis (M.A.)—San Francisco State College, 1951.

Bjorklund, Amy Lord. *A Collections Management Policy for the San Quentin Museum.* San Francisco, CA: San Francisco State University, 1992, 92 p.
Thesis (M.A.)—San Francisco State University, 1992.

Blakely, Thomas Alfred. *An Evaluation of the Administration of the Educational Program at San Quentin Prison.* Berkeley, CA: University of California, Berkeley, 1949, 298 p.
Thesis (Ed.D. in Educational Administration)—University of California, Berkeley, June 1949.

Butler, Roy Everett. *Developing Remedial Academic Education at San Quentin.* Berkeley, CA: University of California, Berkeley, 1959, 69 p.
Seminar paper (School of Education)—University of California, Berkeley, Spring 1959.

Carroll, Catherine S. *The Prison Law Office, San Quentin, California.* Berkeley, CA: University of California, Berkeley, Department of Architecture, 1988, 1 v.
Professional report (Master of Architecture)—University of California, Berkeley, Spring 1988.

Cole, Dennis Eugene. *The 7th Step-Release Class at San Quentin: A Study of Large Group Behavior.* San Francisco, CA: San Francisco State College, 1968, 62 p.
Thesis (M.A.)—San Francisco State College, 1968.

Cummins, Eric F. *Iron Gag: A Chronicle of San Quentin Prison, 1950-1980 Book Suppression, Inmate Resistance, and the Rise and Fall of the Prison Movement Left.* Pennsylvania: University of Pennsylvania, 1990, 614 p.
Thesis (Ph.D.)—University of Pennsylvannia, 1990.

Howard, Harry. *A Study of 1974 Violence in San Quentin: The Perspective of a Protestant Chaplain.* American Baptist Seminary of the West, 1975, 147 p.
Thesis (D. Min.)—American Baptist Seminary of the West, 1975.

LaCombe, Carole Lee. *Newspaper Treatment of Minorities as Reflected in the August, 1971 San Quentin Incident.* San Jose, CA: California State University, San Jose, 1973, 109 p.
Thesis (M.S.)—California State University, San Jose, 1973.

Luster, Walter Leslie. *A Follow-Up Study of Recommendations for Vocational Training in a Penal Institution.* San Francisco, CA: San Francisco State College, 1966, 32 p.
Thesis (M.S.)—San Francisco State College, 1966.

Major, Barbara C. *The Relationship Between Recidivism, Drug History and Participation in Drug Treatment Programs Among State Prison Inmates in the Northern California Reception Center at San Quentin State Prison.*

San Franciso, CA: University of San Francisco, 1992, 119 p.
Thesis (Ed.D., Counseling Psychology Program)—University of San Francisco, 1992.

Nardone, Diane Christine. *The History of the San Quentin Drama Workshop.* New York: New York University, 1978, 214 p.
Thesis (Ph.D.)—New York University, 1978.

Roberts, Earl Leslie, Sr. *A Study of the Effects of Group Counseling on Association Choices and Status Ascription Among Inmates at the California State Prison at San Quentin.* San Francisco, CA: San Francisco State College, 1960, 83 p.
Thesis (M.A.)—San Francisco State College, 1960.

Russell, Bruce Lester, Jr. *A Study of the Knowledge of Prison Operations of Instructors at the California State Prison at San Quentin.* Claremont, CA: Claremont College, 1953, 83 p.
Thesis (M.A.)—Claremont College, 1953.

Schmidt, David Gordon. *An Evaluation of Alcoholics Anonymous at San Quentin Prison.* Stanford, CA: Stanford University, 1945, 233 p.
Thesis (A.M.)—Stanford University, 1945.

Thayer, Ward Havens. *A Comparison of Prison Inmates with Regard to Certain Rehabilitation Factors.* San Francisco, CA: San Francisco State College, 1964, 96 p.
Thesis (M.S.)—San Francisco State College, 1964.

Wright, Eldreadge. *A Follow-Up Study of the Effectiveness of the Vocational Education Program at San Quentin State Prison 1979 Through 1981.* San Francisco, CA: San Francisco State University, 1982, 62 p.
Thesis (M.A.)—San Francisco State University, 1982.

PICTORIAL WORKS

Baltz, Lewis. *Rule Without Exception.* Albuquerque, NM: University of New Mexico Press in Association with the Des Moines Art Center, 1990, 151 p.
"Published in conjunction with the exhibition, 'Lewis Baltz: Rule Without Exception,' organized by Julia Brown Turrell, director of the Des Moines Art Center, Iowa. Includes San Quentin Point by Mark Haworth-Booth."

Baltz, Lewis. *San Quentin Point.* Millerton, NY: Aperture, c1986, 18 p.

Baltz, Lewis. *San Quentin Point: Selections.* New York: Hyperion Press, 1985, 25 photographic prints, silver gelatin, b. & w.; 8" x 10".
Signature, portfolio number, and image numbers in pencil on verso of each photograph. Text by Mark Haworth-Booth. Edition consists of 35 portfolios numbered 1-35, and five artist's proofs numbered I-V. Issued in black wood box with title stencilled on top. Includes title page, three pages of text, notes, and colophon. Castelli Graphic promotional announcement and gallery invitation laid in. Views from and on San Quentin Point, most in line of sight of the prison, some showing prison in distance; includes primarily views depicting marshland, plants, dried mud, and refuse such as boxes, plastic bottles, broken concrete, boards, pipes, and mctal.

Nichols, Nancy Ann. *San Quentin Inside the Walls.* San Quentin, CA: San Quentin Museum Press, 1991, 63 p.

Peek. *This Is San Quentin!: [A Folio of Sketches Depicting the Complete History of the Nation's Largest Prison].* San Quentin, CA: San Quentin Museum Press, 1991, 1 v. unpaged.

AUDIO RECORDINGS

Carr, James Edward. *The View from the End of the World: Live Interviews of Life in Prison with James Carr.* New York: Folkways Records, 1975, 1 sound disk: 33 1/3 rpm; 12 in. + notes. FD 5404; Folkways.
Introduction to cell life in San Quentin—The takeover of D-wing at Soledad—Life in the prison system.

Duffy, Clinton T. *Prisons, Prisoners and Parole.* Los Angeles, CA: Pacifica Tape Library, 1963, 1 cassette 2-track mono. 70 min.
Former Warden Duffy describes the inhuman conditions he encountered and reformed during his administration: the heartbreak of recidivism, and what is being done to make the prisons of the future centers of true rehabilitation.

Ford, Tennessee Ernie. *San Quentin Prison Choir.* Hymns sung by Tennessee Ernie Ford and San Quentin Prison Choir with varying instrumental accompaniment. Recorded at San Quentin Prison. Program notes by Ford and Hal Levy on slipcase.

A Former Convict Talks About the Life of a Parolee. Educational Research Group, 1 cassette. 2-track mono. 24 min., 010 1753. Series: Crime and punishment.
The remarkable life story of a man who moved from baker to bank robber and then to a career as a successful businessman after serving nearly nine years in San Quentin.

Frye, Nickola L. *Nickola Frye, Historian, Talks About San Quentin and the Popularity of the Public Tours Conducted Throughout Its Facility, and About Changes in Her Attitude After Two Years in Residence at San Quentin.* 1 sound tape reel (15 min.): 3 3/4 ips, mono.; 7 in., 1/4 in. tape., 1983.

Inside San Quentin. Los Angeles, CA : Pacifica Tape Library, 1983, 1 sound cassette (13 min.): 1 7/8 ips. Pgm.

no. BC1452. Recorded September 15, 1971 at San Quentin.

A Juvenile Convict Talks About His Entry into a Life of Crime. Educational Research Group, 010 1744.

Moore, Howard. *The San Quentin Six*. Sausalito, CA: n.p., 1974, 1 sound cassette (60 min.): 1 7/8 ips.
Also issued on reel (3 3/4 ips. mono. or stereo. 5 in.). Recorded in Kentfield, CA, April 17, 1974. Focuses on the treatment of a group of prisoners known as the San Quentin Six who were charged with conspiracy and murder. Attorney Howard Moore talks about the legal background of race discrimination, and Fania Davis Jordan describes the physical maltreatment of the San Quentin Six. Terence Hallinan speaks on the prison system.

O'Neal, Joseph M. *Chicano Prisoners: A Discussion and Study Guide*. Austin, TX: Austin Community College, 1979, 1 cassette (c. 30 min.): 1 7/8 ips.+ Notes.
Study notes inserted in container. Designed as a study gude to accompany the book, *Chicano Prisoners: The Key to San Quentin*, by Ted Davidson.

Remember San Quentin. Berkeley, CA: Pacifica Tape Library, 1970/1979, 3 sound cassettes (91 min.): 1 7/8 ips, 2 track, mono. BC 0240—BC 0242 Pacifica.
Report on the deaths at San Quentin Prison on August 21, 1971. In an excape attempt, guards and inmates were killed. An investigation into the incident is discussed by those involved, including wardens, defense attorneys, the District Attorney, and the State Director of Corrections.

Report on the Death of George Jackson. Berkeley, CA: Pacifica Tape Library, 1971, 3 cassettes. 1 cassette. 2-track mono. 24 min. Educational Research Group, 1969.
San Quentin inmate, a former major league pitcher, talks about the antecedents of crime and the impact of prison. He tells of his introduction to and growth in a life of crime,

culminating in murder, for which he is serving a life sentence.

San Quentin Investigation: A Second-Hand View. Los Angeles, CA: Pacifica Tape Library, 1983, 2 sound cassettes (121 min.): 1 7/8 ips. Programme notes in container. Pgm. nos. BC1542a-b.

Clark, John Gee. *John Gee Clark California Legislator, Executive Administrator, and Judge by John Gee Clark: Interviewed by L. Craig Cunningham, Oral History Program, University of California, Los Angeles.* [Los Angeles]: 1966, 219 p.
Transcript of an 11-hour interview completed under the auspices of the UCLA Oral History Program. Studies at the University of California, class of 1913; work as probation officer, Los Angeles; study and practice of law; campaign for state assembly on Democratic ticket, with endorsement of Epic movement; work in the legislature; the 1938 campaign and the Olson administration; director of penology and chairman of board of prison terms and paroles; interest in penal reform; superior court judge. Clark reminisces about his career and activities in California law and politics from 1920-60. Volume includes index. Forms part of: Oral History collection, Dept. of Special Collections, University Library, University of California, Los Angeles.

VIDEO RECORDINGS

Chaplain Ray. *San Quentin Angel.* Dallas, TX: International Prison Ministry, 1987, 1 videocassette (VHS): sd., col.; 1/2 in.
Executive producer, Chaplain Ray; producer, Jan Horton. Videotaped by Flessing and Flessing at San Quentin. Eight former inmates return to San Quentin to witness for Christ at a ceremony presenting the "Angel Award" to Chaplain Ray.

Conditions at San Quentin. Los Angeles, CA: Pacifica Tape Library, 1968, 1 reel (7 in.) 3 3/4 ips. Single track. Pacifica Tape Library 131.

Dead Man Coming. Pyramid Films, Inc., 1973, 24 min. sd. b. & w. 16 mm. With study guide.
Director and editor, Ken Ellis; narrator, Paul Turner; music, Merl Saunders; camera, Jeff Cohen and San Quentin Inmate Film Workshop. Provides insight into life inside a maximum security institution. Inmates and correctional personnel talk about conditions behind the prison walls. Also chronicles the experiences of two inmates who have recently been paroled, and shows how incarceration has affected their lives. Filmed at San Quentin State Prison.

Harkness, Richard. *Inside San Quentin*. Novato, CA: Marin Community Video, 1976, 2 cassettes, 90 min.: sd., col. ; 3/4 in.
Views of the inmates and personnel of San Quentin. Day to day life and programs in San Quentin.

San Quentin Drama Workshop. *En Attendant Godot* [videorecording] / une co-production, Caméras Continentales... [*et al.*]; réalisation, Walter D. Asmus. Paris: Vision Seuil, c1988, 1 videocassette (140 min.) : sd., col. ; 1/2 in. VHS SECAM.
Cast: Jean-François Balmer, Jean-Pierre Jorris, Roman Polanski, Rufus, Philippe Deschamps. Credits: Director of photography, Daniel Vogel. A performance of the San Quentin Drama Workshop. Presented by the University of Maryland, College Park, Visual Press and Caméras Continentales. Summary: A presentation of the definitive version, as he directed it, of Samuel Beckett's absurd play in which his non-heroes, Didi and Gogo, wait and hope for Godot. Language: French.

San Quentin Drama Workshop. *La Dernière Bande* [videorecording] / une co-production, Caméras Continentales... [*et al.*]; producteurs délégues, Jean-Pierre

Cottet, Mitchell Lifton; réalisation, Walter D. Asmus. Paris: Vision Seuil, c1988, 1 videocassette (54 min.) : sd., col. ; 1/2 in. VHS format (SECAM).
Cast: Roland Bertin. Credits: Director of photography, Daniel Vogel. A performance of the San Quentin Drama Workshop. Presented by the University of Maryland, College Park, Visual Press and Caméras Continentales. Summary: A presentation of the definitive version, as he directed it, of Beckett's one-man play with a tape recorder. Language: French.

San Quentin Drama Workshop. *Endgame* [videorecording] / by Samuel Beckett; a co-production of the Visual Press of the University of Maryland at College Park, the Division of Video Programs of the Smithsonian Institution Press, and the San Quentin Drama Workshop; producer, William Gilcher; directed for the stage by Samuel Beckett; directed for the film by Robert Bilheimer. Black and white version. Washington, DC: Smithsonian Video Library, c1992, 1 videocassette (96 min.): sd., b. &w.; 1/2 in. VHS format (NTSC).
Cast: Bud Thorpe, Rick Cluchey, Teresita Garcia Suro. Credits: Director of photography, Ron Mix; editor, David H. Rose. Summary: The San Quentin Drama Workshop presents an English version of Beckett's play *Fin de partie*. Language: English.

San Quentin Drama Workshop. *Krapp's Last Tape* [videorecording] / by Samuel Beckett; a co-production of Caméras Continentales... [*et al.*]; produced by Mitchell Lifton and Jean-Pierre Cottet; directed by Walter D. Asmus. Washington, DC: Smithsonian Institution Press, c1990, 1 videocassette (46 min.) : sd., col. ; 1/2 in. VHS format.
Cast: Rick Cluchey. Credits: Director of photography, Daniel Vogel; cameramen, Tom Arnold, Francis Guilbert, Jean-Marc Zilbering; editor, Christian Martin. A performance of the San Quentin Drama Workshop. Presented by the University of Maryland, College Park,

Visual Press and Caméras Continentales. Summary: A presentation of the definitive version, as he directed it, of Beckett's one-man play with a tape recorder. Language: English.

San Quentin Drama Workshop. *Waiting for Godot* videorecording / a co-production of Caméras Continentales... [*et al.*]; produced by Mitchell Lifton and Jean-Pierre Cottet; directed by Walter D. Asmus. Washington, DC: Smithsonian Video Library, c1990, 2 videocassettes (137 min.) : sd., col.; 1/2 in. VHS format [NTSC].

Cast: Lawrence Held, Bud Thorpe, Alan Mandell, Rick Cluchey, Louis Beckett Cluchey. Credits: Director of photography, Daniel Vogel; cameramen, Luc Herve... [*et al.*]. A performance of the San Quentin Drama Workshop. Presented by the University of Maryland, College Park, Visual Press and Caméras Continentales. Summary: A presentation of the definitive version, based on the notes of Samuel Beckett, of his absurd play in which his non-heroes, Didi and Gogo, wait and hope for Godot. Language: English.

***Squires of San Quentin*.** Schiller Park, IL: Motorola Teleprograms, 1978, 1 reel, 30 min.: sd., col.; 16 mm. J. Gary Mitchell Film Co.

Deals with workshops for adolescent, delinquent boys sponsored by the inmates of San Quentin Prison. Uses *cinéma vérité* footage to capture group meetings where conversation centers in a comparison of the youths' and the convicts' actions in order to encourage the boys to become introspective. Shows a mixed group of juvenile delinquents in open and constructive workshops with the "Squires," an organization of long-term inmates at San Quentin whose mission is to counsel young people who have started on the criminal spiral.

MOTION PICTURES

The Big House. 84 min., b. & w. M.G.M., 1930.
Stars Chester Morris, Wallace Beery, Lewis Stone, Robert Montgomery, and Leila Hyams. Directed by George Hill. Story and dialogue by Frances Marion. Based on the book by a former San Quentin inmate. *Variety* called it a "...virile, realistic melodrama..." *The New York Times* said "It is an insight into life in a jail that has never before been essayed on the screen."

Duffy of San Quentin. 78 min., b. & w. Warner Bros. Pictures, 1954.
Stars Louis Hayward, Joanne Dru, and Paul Kelly. Co-stars Maureen O'Sullivan. Directed by Walter Doniger. Screenplay by Walter Doniger. From a story by Berman Swarttz and Walter Doniger based on the book *The San Quentin Story*, by Clinton T. Duffy. Duffy becomes Warden of San Quentin and introduces reforms. A hardened convict becomes a new man when he falls in love with a beautiful nurse. *Variety* called it "...a slow-moving prison melodrama, developed in ordinary fashion, and there is very little of interest, even for undiscriminating audiences..." *The New York Times* said of the romantic interest "...it looks like the silliest sort of eyewash in the most hackneyed sort of prison film."

I Want to Live. 120 min., 1958.
Stars Susan Hayward. Directed by Robert Wise, screenplay by Nelson Gilling and Don M. Mankiewicz, based on articles by Ed Montgomery and letters of Barbara Graham. A real-life drama of the last years of Barbara Graham, a woman convicted of prostitution, perjury, forgery, and murder, who was sentenced to die in San Quentin's gas chamber. *Variety* said that the movie "...may be prevented by its grim honesty from being a blockbuster, nothing can stop it from being a bombshell....the most damning indictment of capital punishment ever documented in any medium." *The New*

York Times said that Susan Hayward had "...never done anything so vivid or so shattering to an audience's nerves..."

On the Yard. 102 min., color. 1979.
Stars John Heard, Thomas D. Waites, and Mike Kellin. Directed by Raphael Silver, screenplay by Malcolm Braly, based on the novel *On the Yard*, by Malcolm Braly. Leonard Maltin, noted film historian, said: "So-so prison picture seems hardly worth the effort, though Kellin is memorable as an aging loser trying to get paroled."

San Quentin. 66 min., b. & w., RKO, 1946.
Stars Lawrence Tierney. Directed by Gordon M. Douglas, screenplay by Lawrence Kimble, Arthur A. Ross, and Howard J. Green. Warden Kelly trys to keep his prisoners' welfare league going despite opposition. He travels with a group of prisoners to San Francisco to speak to a newspaper club, but a convict turns on him and others while escaping. *Variety* said this film "...stacks up as a near-documentary with plenty of interest for the melodrama market..." and that it has "...plenty of movement, spotting action and development without a slow moment." *The New York Times* said that "...the yarn about an ex-prisoner and founder of San Quentin's Inmates Welfare League, whose good work is nearly wrecked by an escaped killer, strays from its noble intentions to settle down to a traditional manhunt. From there on the going is normal, prosaic and only occasionally exciting." Furthermore, "...though former Warden Lewis E. Lawes of Sing Sing sounds a note of approval in the prologue, 'San Quentin' can hardly be listed as a documentary."

San Quentin. 70 min., b. & w., Warner Brothers. 1937.
Stars Pat O'Brien, Humphrey Bogart, and Ann Sheridan. Directed by Lloyd Bacon, screenplay by Peter Milne and Humphrey Cobb, based on a story by Robert Tasker and John Bright. A convict's sister falls in love with the captain of the prison yard, the very man the convict feels has wronged him. *Variety* said this film "...is stark, authentic-looking prison

melodrama that misses being big entertainment because of a love story that is none too strong and a plot that is only moderately forceful." *The New York Times* called it "...another of those Warner Brothers screen parables of prison life, this one dealing entertainingly enough and briskly, too, with the rehabilitation of a misanthropic mug named Red Kennnedy."

The Steel Cage. 86 min., b. & w., released by United Artists Corp., 1954.
Stars Paul Kelly, Maureen O'Sullivan, Walter Slezak, John Ireland, Lawrence Tierney, Kenneth Tobey, and Arthur Franz. Directed by Walter Doniger. Based on the book *The San Quentin story*, by Clinton T. Duffy and Dean Jennings. Three episodes of prison life reflect the desire of prisoners for comedy, freedom, and religious solace. In "The Chef" a group of convicts frames a prison cook after his release, and returns him to jail because they like his cooking. "The Hostage" depicts an unsuccessful jail break attempt in which the ringleaders die violently. In "The Face" an agnostic prisoner artist finds spiritual solace when he restores a religious painting in the chapel. *Variety* said that the "...entertainment is spotty and slowly paced..."

TELEVISION SHOWS

KTLA News. KTLA news, Los Angeles, California. 1971-08-25 excerpt and/or out takes. San Quentin, SM3565. 1971-08-25. 1 roll of col. 16 mm. *News of the Day*. [Vol. 33, no. 267—excerpt. 5 convicts captured after break from San Quentin Prison]. [1962-03-30].
"Barking of a housewife's dog results in the capture of fugitives who staged first wall-scaling break in 19 years"—Hearst index card. Shot description: Prison (long shot). Wall (long shot). Pan shot same. Warden holding rope and talking to press. Rope (closeup). Man looks at ground. Foot prints (closeup). Guards looking. Same (AA). Same (AA). Prisoner in yard. Prisoner walks in. Prisoners sitting. Same (AA). Closing gates. Same (closeup) (Hearst index card).

On the Go. San Quentin. 1959 or 1960. Host: Jack Linkletter.

"On the Go" began on April 27, 1959 and lasted until July 8, 1960. It was a half-hour variety show airing at 10 A.M., Monday through Friday on CBS. One of the earlier episodes was filmed at San Quentin.

San Quentin. 45 min., 1970. Produced by Lane Community College Media Productions, Eugene, OR.

Broadcast as an episode of *The Merv Griffin Show*. Off-air licensing rights through the Television Licensing Center. Griffin conducts an interview on prison life and prison reform with Louis Nelson, San Quentin's Warden; John Marr, director and founder of Delancey Street Project in San Francisco; and Donald Cressey, University of California at Santa Barbara professor and prison reform authority. Presents opposing viewpoints on the present penal system that works against rehabilitation and a system that assists the prisoner to become a productive member of society.

San Quentin: Some Views from the Outside. 30 min. With Dick Shoemaker. Aired 12-13-72, ABC, as a companion piece to *Truman Capote at San Quentin*.

A panel of three California penal experts commented on Truman Capote's efforts and addressed some of the issues raised. *Variety* reported that the experts agreed "...prisons do not work in current society and the most promising alternative is a community approach towards smaller convict facilities within individual population areas."

Truman Capote at San Quentin. 90 min. An episode of *On Location*. Aired 12-13-72, ABC.

Said *Variety*, "Truman Capote's 90 minutes inside San Quentin Prison talking to six or so prisoners provided rather engrossing viewing....the subjects included a two-time inhabitant of death row, a homosexual con, a two-time wife killer (and prison newspaper editor), a drug spree killer, a rapist who had since married while in prison, and a member of the Charles Manson Family."

Archival Materials

Byrne. Letter to Antonio Maria Melendres: San Francisco: ALS, 1854 Dec. 23, 2 p.
Draft, concerning construction of road to the Embarcadero of San Quentin. Forms part of the Robert Ernest Cowan Collection.

Dale, Jimmie. *Eighteen Years in Prison: This Booklet Contains the Prison Experience of Jimmie Dale: "Man's Inhumanity to Man Makes Countless Thousands Mourn."* Los Angeles, CA: n.p., 1920s?, 8 p.

The Death Penalty: The Men Who Have Suffered It at San Quentin Prison: Their Lives and Crimes Briefly Sketched. S.n.: S.l., 1903, 107 p.

Duffy, Clinton T. *Papers*. 1940-1951, 10 linear ft.
Correspondence, photographs, writings, and publications by Duffy and others, reflecting his service as Warden of San Quentin Prison and his sentiments in favor of prison reform and against capital punishment.

Fox, Edward T. *Story of the Issuance of Book III, San Quentin Prison, July 28, 1946* [*i.e.*, War ration book III]. San Francisco, CA: 1946, 23 p.

G.S.G. *A Prison Bookshelf: Thirty Book Reviews*. San Quentin, CA: Vocation Print Shop, 1949, 118 p.
"Reprinted from the *San Quentin News*, San Quentin, California." Owned by the University of California, Berkeley's Bancroft Library.

Helsing, Oswald E. *Emil Marcussen: Biographical Sketch.* 1938, 9 leaves.

Concerning his early life on the sea; his conversion to the Salvation Army, ca. 1887; his career in the Salvation Army in Denmark and in the U.S., including his work as chaplain at San Quentin.

Hoyle, John E. *Papers Relating to San Quentin Prison.* Circa 1907-1913, 5 boxes, 2 oversize folders.
Collection contains correspondence both from within and outside the prison, reports, a 1913 transcript of an investigation, writings and drawings, mainly by prisoners, programs of prison entertainments, and other miscellaneous materials. San Quentin collection of Roy Groves.

Jackson, Georgia. *Communication on Human Rights by Georgia Jackson* (mother of slain prisoner George Jackson)...[*et al.*]. S.l.: the authors, 1971, 19 p.

Lamott, Kenneth Church. *Papers.* 1950-1975. 15.5 cubic ft. (32 boxes).
Contains correspondence (1956-75); subject files used to write his books on San Quentin Prison and the murder trial of Laura D. Fair (1950-1975); and the manuscripts for several of his books. Lamott (1923-1979) was an editor, free-lance writer, and author. *Anti-California* manuscript, *Escape from Stress* manuscript, *Chronicles of San Quentin* manuscript.

Mooney Pamphlet Collection: miscellaneous material on Tom Mooney. 1916-1940, 3 boxes.
Connection of certain Department of Labor employees with the case of Thomas J. Mooney. 1919: The story of Mooney and Billings. 1928: Governor Young, pardon Tom Mooney... 1929: The amazing frameup of Mooney and Billings / Marcet Haldeman-Julius. 1931: frameup of Mooney and Billings / Marcet Haldeman-Julius. 1931: Tom Mooney... betrayed by labor leaders. 2d ed. 1931: In the matter of the application made on behalf of Thomas J. Mooney for a pardon. 1932: The Mooney-Billings report. 1932: Our American Dreyfus case / by Lillian Symes. 1935: In the

matter of the application of Thomas J. Mooney for a writ of habeas corpus (Criminal no. 3898) 1935. 3 v.: Senate daily journal, California Legislature... Mar. 16, 1937: California decisions... Nov. 4, 1937: Thomas J. Mooney, petitioner, against Court Smith, Warden of San Quentin... 1937-1938. 3 v.: Hearing... Smith, Warden of San Quentin... 1937-1938. 3 v.: Hearing...of the Committee on the Judiciary...on S.J. Res. 127. 1938: Tom Mooney's message. 1938: We accuse / by Vito Marcantonio. 1938: Hearings...of the Committee on the Judiciary...on H.J. Res. 297. 1938: Radio address of Hon. Emanuel Celler...May 28, 1938: A San Franciscan tells the story of the Mooney case / H.C. Carrasco. 1938: Justice is waiting 1940: [Material from the Tom Mooney Molders' Defense Committee, copies of legal documents and letters, pamphlets, newspaper and magazine articles, extracts of the Congressional record] articles, extracts of the Congressional record]. Mooney, Thomas J., 1882-1942. In the matter of the application of Thomas J. Mooney for a writ of habeas corpus. 1935. Marcantonio, Vito, 1902-1954. We accuse. 1938. Symes, Lillian, 1895- Our American Dreyfus case. 1935. Carrasco, H. C. San Franciscan tells the story of the Mooney, 1938. Haldeman-Julius, Marcet, 1887-1941.

The Open Door: Reedosophy and extracts from letters written by members of Samuel Payne Reed's classes in San Quentin State Prison, California, and the federal prison on Alcatraz Island... San Francisco, CA: S. P. Reed, 1927, 40 p.

Oppenheimer, Jake. *Softening the Heart of a Convict.* Oakland, CA: E. Morrell, c1912, 15 p. Jake Oppenheimer, called "The Prison Tiger," describes his first experience with the straightjacket, in which he was tortured for 110 hours.

Scudder, Kenyon J(udson), interviewee. Kenyon J. Scudder criminologist and social engineer, interviewed by Donald J. Schippers, 1965. Los Angeles, CA: Oral

History Program, University of California, Los Angeles, 1967, [4], iii, 508 leaves, bound.
Transcript of a 14.75-hour interview completed under the auspices of the UCLA Oral History Program. Scudder discusses his innovations in the fields of corrections and social engineering. Forms part of: Oral History Collection, Dept. of Special Collections, University Library, University of California, Los Angeles.

Shafter, Payne J. *Payne J. Shafter Papers, 1876-1894.* 1 portfolio.
Include letters to him from California State Prison at San Quentin and from Robert Dollar re his supplying them with wood, and from the California State Board of Agriculture re reward for his gelding, Viking; accounts. From the W. Scott Polland Collection.

Snodgrass, Marion Myers. *M. M. Snodgrass: Memories of the Richmond-San Rafael Ferry Company: An Interview Conducted by Judith K. Dunning in 1985.* Berkeley, CA: Regional Oral History Office, The Bancroft Library, University of California, c1992, [17], 75, [4] leaves, [3] leaves of plates: ports.

Stanley, Leo Leonidas. *Papers.* 15 boxes (including 39 v.). 1928-1965.
Descriptions, with photos, of trips taken by Stanley as ship's doctor (14 v.), American prisons he visited (3 v.), and a meeting he attended in 1965 (1 v.); together with manuscript novel of a prisoner, J. P. Watson (1 v.) and other papers, including account (4 p.) of Stanley's experiences during the San Francisco earthquake and fire of 1906. Stanley was the physician for San Quentin Prison, 1913-51.

Stanley, Leo Leonidas. *San Quentin Prison Photographs.* 1 album. 1912-1920.
Compiled by longtime chief medical officer at San Quentin Prison. Bequest of Dr. Leo L. Stanley via the *Marin Independent Journal*.

The State Prison: San Quentin Prison. Photostat from *California Police Gazette*. San Francisco, CA: California Police Gazette, 1859, 5 p.

Stebbins, William P. C. *William P. C. Stebbins Papers, 1853-1857*. 5 folders in portfolio. 1853-1857.
Papers relating to Stebbins' lawsuit against the San Francisco Manufacturing Company concerning the construction of the State Prison at San Quentin; with accounts and payrolls. Forms part of the Thomas W. Norris Collection.

Stereoscopic Views of Marin County, California, 1865-1872. 11 stereographs (photoprints): albumen, b. & w.; 87 x 177mm. 3 stereographs (photoprints): albumen, b. & w.; 100 x 177 mm. 3 stereographs (photoprints): silver gelatin, b. & w.; 90 x 180mm.
Includes views by Carleton E. Watkins, Eadweard Muybridge, Keystone View Company, and other photographers and publishers. Views of Marin County, California, including San Quentin and San Rafael, Point Bonita, and Mt. Tamalpais: includes views of the state prison, a steamboat landing, general views of San Rafael, views of the court house, a bank, hotels, homes, farms, and cattle grazing on a hillside; view of Mt. Tamalpais from Sausalito shows hills and farms; a view of Point Bonita shows road along a rocky headland leading to the lighthouse on the southernmost extremity of the county.

View of the Ferry Landing Near San Quentin/San Rafael. 1 photoprint. San Quentin, CA: 1951.
Photograph taken from the deck of a ferry. Mount Tamalpais looms in the background.

Wells, Fargo & Company. *$100 Reward: Escaped from the States Prison at San Quentin, Cal., July 17th, 1875, Wm. Harrington...* 1 broadside, 31 x 45 cm. San Francisco, CA: Wells, Fargo & Company, 1875. Signed: Jno. J. Valentine, Gen. Supt.

Yale, Gregory. *Legal Papers of Gregory Yale*: consisting of briefs, complaints, writs, court records, letters, memoranda, etc. connected with Yale's practice as attorney in various mining and land cases, and for the Pilots association of San Francisco. San Francisco: 1850-1869, 2 boxes, 1 oversize portfolio.

Typewritten lists of their contents included in vols. 1 and 2. Part of the original manuscript of Yale's Mining claims and water rights; Glossaries; Yale's protest in the matter of widening Kearney street; Notes by Yale on the right to tax persons living on public lands. Also includes letters from Joshua Hamblin, George C. Yount, and William Early Jones (in portfolio). Contents.- v. 1. Limantour claim; New Almaden mine.- v. 2. Peter Smith land titles; California vs. Randall, Holden and Swett; Original drafts of California mining law.- v. 3. San Francisco pilots association cases, 1850-69.- v. 4. San Quentin Prison case (James M. Estell); Sepulveda and Larco vs. Gabriel Maldonado (Comstock Lode)- v. 5 Miscellaneous cases: Slander suit of Comerford vs. DeVries, 1857; W. Blanding vs. E.W. Burr et al., Board of fund commissioners, 1859; Rancho Pastoria de las Borregas (J.M. Estrada vs. Castro and Murphy, 1859-65; Cole's ranch in San Francisco, 1860-61; Halleck et al., executors of Folsom vs. J. Mora Moss and the Sacramento Valley railroad, 1861; Sonora company's notice of location, 1862; General land office re Soscal rancho, 1863; Brief history of Sausalito and the title of Guillermo Antonio Richardson, 1867; Mesick vs. Brannan et al; A translation of the Spanish laws in existence during the time of Philip II of Spain relating to the taxes of free Negroes and mulattos; Abstract of the title of the Rancho Punta de los Reyes (Andrew Randall); Document 13, New Almaden Mine.

Yale, Gregory. *State v McCauly: Minutes of Argument on Application for Injunction, Aug. 1860* [manuscript]. 1859, 160 p.

Gregory Yale (1816-1871), a prominent San Francisco lawyer, defended John McCauley and Lloyd Tevis in the case, State of California vs. John F. McCauley and Lloyd

Tevis ("State Prison Case") in August of 1859. Holograph notebook containing notes made by Yale between August 17th and August 19th, 1859 concerning the trial.

Maps

California State Prison, at San Quentin. Clinton T. Duffy, warden; H.O. Simpson, Supt. of Maintenance & Construction; cartography: C. Murray, April 2, 1946. Rev. 1950. Photo reprod.; 51 x 87 cm. San Quentin, CA: C. Murray, 1950.

Scale [1:2, 400] 1"= 200'. (W 122p0s28/N37p0s56). Blueprint. Shows buildings, gun towers, fences, etc. Also shows town of San Quentin.

IV.

SAN QUENTINIANA

BOOKS PUBLISHED BY OFFICIALS AND INMATES OF SAN QUENTIN

by Herman K. Spector

OCTOBER, 1953

This compilation of an annotated bibliography of books published by officials and former inmates of San Quentin was inspired by our good friend and colleague, Austin H. McCormick, Professor, School of Criminology, University of California. The setting from which this suggestion came was a course in problems in correctional administration which Professor McCormick presented in the spring of 1953 for the administrative staff at San Quentin. He felt that, in this literature, there would be much of interest to those engaged in correctional work. Moreover, in reading these books, personnel of the California correctional service would gain a good perspective on the history of penology in this state.

The careful work of Herman K. Spector, Senior Librarian of the institution is reflected in the preparation of this bibliography.

—H. O. Teets,
Warden

Black, Jack. *You Can't Win*, with a foreword by Robert Herrick. New York: Macmillan, 1926, 394 p.

These experiences are written by a man who spent 15 years in the cannister for burglary and robbery, and who, after 28 years of crime, reinstated himself in society. Harry Elmer Barnes, in his *New Horizons in Criminology*, evaluates one of those essays thusly: "Perhaps the best revelations of the mental attitudes of the habitual criminal ever set forth in brief form." Summing up his own criminal philosophy, Black says: "I learned the lesson of violence in prison, and I believe that I lived in a world of violence, had to use violence, and use it first. I had no more thought of right or wrong than a wolf that prowls the prairie. I hunted because I was hunted myself, and I showed no consideration for anybody or anything because I knew I would receive none. I had formed the criminal habit. Habit is the strongest thing in life, and [professional] criminals obey the impulse to commit crime almost subconsciously."

OFFICIAL PRISON RECORD

Received San Quentin 12/18/12 as #26196, Black, John; from San Francisco County for the crime of assault to robbery for sentence of one year. Discharged 10/28/13. Received Folsom 10/10/1898 as #4490 from San Francisco County for crime of felony for sentence of eight years. Alias: Jack Black; H. J. Kline.

Booth, Ernest G. *Ladies of the Big House* (a photoplay about San Quentin). 8 reels, sound; from the play by Ernest Booth. United States Copyright Office, December 26, 1931, Paramount Publix Corporation. The article entitled "Ladies in Durance Vile," in the *American Mercury* 22 (April, 1931): 392-402, may have been the original basis for this play.

OFFICIAL PRISON RECORD

Received San Quentin 10/7/17 as #30975, Booth, Ernest G., from Butte County for crime of forgery for indeterminate sentence of 1-14 years. Out to court 3/19/18 on Supreme Court order declaring sentence null and void. Returned 3/28/18 as #31494 for the same offense for a sentence of 5 years. Released on parole 4/27/20. Declared violator 12/18/20. Returned to San Quentin 1/19/21. Transferred to Folsom 1/30/23 as #12412. Discharged 4/24/23. Received Folsom 11/23/24 as #13332, Booth, Ernest, from Alameda County for crime of robbery first degree and pr/fel for sentence of 5 years to life. Transferred to Folsom 7/12/27. Paroled 8/23/37. Discharged 2/23/40. Received San Quentin 11/8/47 as #A7557, Booth, Ernest Granville, from Los Angeles County for the crime of robbery first two counts and two pr/fel for sentence of 5 years to life two counts concurrent. Federal commitment received 11/14/47 for 15 years and 5 years consecutive and concurrent with state sentence. Transferred to Terminal Island 7/22/50.

Booth, Ernest G. *Stealing Through Life*. New York: Alfred A. Knopf, 1927, 308 p.
The story of a bank robber who, at the age of 16, received his first "break" from an Oakland juvenile courtroom. In the preface the author states, "The pages which follow constitute an effort to work out the fundamental causes which brought me to prison. I do not want to appear in the light of attempting to justify my present position. But if the so-called 'crime-wave' is due to such criminals as I have met, both official and in the 'underworld,' then to claim that wave and give to it the tranquillity the reformers moan for is but a matter of intelligent application of simple changes which, I believe, are all too obvious."

Booth, Ernest G. *With Sirens Screaming*. Garden City, NY: Doubleday & Co., 1945, 294 p.
Two young people in love run into difficulties in their attempts to get married. They get entangled with the law. The man lands in a California prison with a long sentence. In prison, more bad luck overtakes him, and while there is an

interlude of happiness, the end of the story is inevitable tragedy. *The New York Times Book Review* said: "His story has just enough plausibility, beyond its grim San Quentin authenticity, to make it at times an almost terrifying experience."

Duffy, Clinton T., with Dean Jennings. *San Quentin Story.* Garden City, NY: Doubleday & Co., 1950, 255 p.

The English edition was published in 1951 by Peter Davies, and was very favorably reviewed in the *Howard Journal* 8 (1952): 212-213. The contents of this book were first serialized in the *Saturday Evening Post* from March 25 through May 13, 1950. The American pocket book edition was published in 1951. The German edition, *Zuchthaus in San Francisco,* was completed in 1951 by Wolfgang Metzner Verlag, and contained several excellent illustrations as an appendix. Written by the man who was Warden of San Quentin from 1940-51, and who presently is one of the members of the California State Adult Authority. The prominent newspaper, *Springfield Republican*, in its issue of June 25, 1950 declared: "The Warden of San Quentin tells of the early days at San Quentin, when Tom Mooney was the best-known prisoner there, and when riots, prison breaks, and daring excapes were frequent occurrences. In addition to these stories, Warden Duffy also reports on the many reforms which he has carried out, and which have made him one of the county's leading penological experts." Mr. Joseph Henry Jackson, the distinguished book reviewer of the *San Francisco Chronicle*, evaluated this book (July 9, 1950) thusly: "A wholly lively and dramatic narrative by an expert. As it happens, I've been in a position to read a rather large proportion of everything Dean Jennings has written in the last decade or so, and I have no hesitation about saying that this book, both technically and 'humanly,' if I may put it that way, is the best writing job he's ever done."

Ford, Tirel L. *California State Prisons: Their History, Development, and Management.* James K. Barry, 1910, 78 p., charts, maps, photos, tabs.

Contents: Foreword; Introduction; The Problem Presented; The Prisons We Started With; The First State Prison; The Prison Located at San Quentin; Inadequacy of the Buildings; Criminal Law in the Fifties; The State Takes Over the Prison; The Prison and Prisoners Again Leased; Abominable Prison Conditions; The State Again Resumes Control; Prison Labor; The Control of Prisoners; The State Prison at Folsom; The Present Prison Plants; Inadequacy of Present Prison Plants; Present Sanitary Conditions Good; The New Buildings and Plans; Legal Machinery for Prison Administration; The Average Prisoner (some statistical data); The Criminal Insane; The Modern Treatment of Convicts; Essential Features of the New Penology; California One of the Advanced States; Credits for Good Behavior; The Parole System; What the Parole System Is; California Has Yet Much to Do; The Reformatory; A Question of State Policy; The Indeterminate Sentence; Classification of Prisoners; Conclusion.

Johnston, James A. *Prison Life Is Different.* Boston: Houghton Mifflin Co., 1937, 337 p., illus.

The author was Warden of San Quentin from 1913-24. Contents: I Suddenly Become Warden; Hell Breaks Loose; The Human Hyena; Big Breaks and Little Breaks; Fresh Air for Foul; Convicts Tell Me Their Troubles; Warden of Two Prisons; From Folsom to San Quentin; Difficulty of Classifying Criminals; Convicts in Kaleidoscope; Individualization in Treatment; Criminality Overlapped by Insanity; Battered and Bruised Humanity in Need of Repair; Listening to Prisoners; Hope; Jute Mill; Training for Living; The Morning Mail; Replacing Ignorance With Knowledge; The Way Parole Works; Old Time Cases and Modern Types; Mooney, Billings, the McNamara Brothers, and Other Dynamiters; "Big Bill," "Bluebeard," "The Confessor," "The Count," "Peg Leg"—How He Operated and How He Was Captured; The Female of the Species; Who Are the Lawless?; Innocent Man Shanghaied Into Prison; William Jennings Bryan Talks About Opportunity; Experts Study the Prison and Prisoners; Sarah Bernhardt and Other Celebrities

Relieve Monotony; Ingenious Plots to Escape; Outside Looking in vs. Inside Looking Out; Negro Convict Who Was a Good Sport; A Question About the Morality of War; I Saw Them Die on the Gallows; Train a Child in the Way He Should Go.

Krebs, Richard Julius Herman (Jan Valtin, pseudonym). *Bend in the River and Other Stories*, with an Introduction by Pat Gil Rankin. Alliance Book Company, 1942, 281 p. Short stories and sketches written while the author was a prisoner in San Quentin, where he wrote for the prison paper, *The San Quentin Bulletin.* Drake De Kay, in his *New York Times Book Review*, says, "While not glossing over serious defects in California's penal system, Valtin makes it abundantly clear in his comments why after his release and deportation, he should have found life in Germany unendurable."

OFFICIAL PRISON RECORD

Received San Quentin 10/3/26 as #42785, Krebs, Richard, from Los Angeles County for the crime of assault with a deadly weapon for 0-10 years. Paroled 12/5/29. Discharged 4/23/33. Granted full and unconditional pardon by Governor Olson 11/30/41.

Krebs, Richard Julius Herman (Jan Valtin, pseudonym). *Out of the Night*. Alliance Book Company, 1951, 841 p.. The title of this startling autobiography is taken from the first line of William Henry's famour poem, "Invictus." According to San Quentin Prison records, this author was born in Dormstadt, Germany on December 17, 1905. He worked in the institution's jute mill for three years and contributed many articles to the inmate publication, *The San Quentin Bulletin.*

Lamson, David Albert. *We Who Are About to Die: Prison as Seen by a Condemned Man.* New York: Charles Scribner's Sons, 1935, 338 p.

"In 1935 when [the author] was employed as a sales manager for the Stanford Press, he was accused, tried, and convicted for the murder of his wife. On appeal the Supreme Court reversed the decision and a new trial was ordered. In the meantime Lamson spent 13 months in Condemned Row in San Quentin Prison. This book is a record of his observations of men and methods in prison life."—*Book Review Digest*. *The New York Times Book Review* calls this book "...not only a social document of considerable importance, but also an honest narrative ably written which cannot fail to hold the interest."

OFFICIAL PRISON RECORD

Received San Quentin 10/6/33 as #54761, Lamson, David, from Santa Clara County for the crime of murder first degree under sentence of death. Out to Superior Court, Santa Clara County 11/14/34 for retrial and discharged on above sentence. Results of retrial—acquittal.

London, Jack. *Star Rover*. New York: Macmillan, 1914, 329 p.

This book is considered unlike anything else that London ever wrote. It is the story of a man in prison who sets free his soul by letting it wander back through former lives. It has often been said that Jack London's men act like animals and that his animals act like men. This powerful story is also full of the primitive. He wrote this after his return from Japan. At that time he declared, "I became a tramp, begging my way from door to door, wandering over the United States and sweating bloddy sweats in slums and in prisons. At the age of eighteen I was down in the cellar of society."—(From his *What Life Means to Me*).

Confined in solitary and doomed to such tortures in the straitjacket as make the rack and rope of the middle ages seem gentle by contrast, Darnell Standing, a lifer in San Quentin Prison, found that he could free his soul from his body and escape form the house of pain to go winging off thru space and time. Ed Morrell, a fellow lifer, told him the secret: "The trick is to die in the jacket, to will yourself to die...you lie on your back as comfortable as you can get, and you begin to use your will. You begin with the toes, one at time. Once you've got the first toe dead, the rest is easy. When your body is all dead, and you are all there yet, you just skin out and leave your body. Stone walls and iron doors are to hold bodies in."

The story has two lines of interest. One follows Standing's adventures after he had learned to carry out Morrell's injunctions and willed his body to die. In a series of episodes, he relives his past in previous incarnations. The other lies in the book's terrible revelation of what imprisonment means.

OFFICIAL PRISON RECORD

Jacob Oppenheimer may be the prisoner on which the character of Darnell Standing is based. Received at Folsom 8/15/1897 as #3545, Oppenheimer, Jacob, from Alameda County for the crime of robbery. Transferred to San Quentin 2/2/1899 as #18056 with additonal commitment from Sacramento County for crime of murder second degree for a sentence of death, and from Marin County for the crime of assault with a deadly weapon causing death while serving life sentence. Executed 7/11/13.

Lowrie, Donald. *My Life in Prison.* New York: Mitchell Kennerley, 1912, 422 p.

This is what he wrote, for example, of the jute mill—"It was an inferno where men with faces painfully drawn to a tensity strove miserably amid the jarring roar to perform the weekly task. The alternative was to spend Saturday and Sunday in the dungeon..."

OFFICIAL PRISON RECORD

Received San Quentin 7/24/01 as #19093, Lowrie, C. D., from Los Angeles County for the crime of burglary for a sentence of 5 years. Discharged 2/13/05. Received San Quentin 11/13/06 as #21873, Lowrie, C. D., from Alameda County for the crime of burglary first degree for a sentence of 15 years. Paroled 8/1/11. Pardoned 1/2/13. Aliases: Donald Lawrie, C. D. Lawrie, Arthur Townsend, James J. Jamison.

Morrell, Ed, and Mildred Ward. *Twenty-Fifth Man: The Strange Story of Ed Morrell, the Hero of Jack London's Star Rover, Lone Survivor of the Famous Band of California Feud Outlaws.* Foreword by George W. P. Hunt, introduction by Raymond S. Ward. New Era Publishing Co., 1924, 390.

Detailed descriptions of his experiences at San Quentin and Folsom.

OFFICIAL PRISON RECORD

Received San Quentin 3/27/1891 as #14486, Martin, Edward, from San Bernardino County for the crime of grand larceny for sentence of 2.5 years. Discharged 3/27/1893. Received Folsom 4/17/1894 as #3097, Morrell, Ed, from Fresno County for the crime of robbery and prior for sentence of life. Transferred to San Quentin 5/18/1896 as #16766. Commuted by Lt. Governor Porter on 3/12/1908. Discharged 3/14/1908.

Odlum, Jerome. *Each Dawn I Die.* Indianapolis: Bobbs-Merrill Co., 1938, 291 p.

One critic described this as "...a prison tale and a superior one. It is written swiftly and cleanly and has a stout heart, a gentle spirit, and a lot of common sense to it...it's only a slight tale, but it touches on the stuff of universality. It rings the bell cleanly." Austin MacCormick said, "Hollywood might well be interested, for here is a script for another thin, super-claptrap prison...The novel has at least two good parts—the leading characters talk like real prisoners and there is an occasional bit of description...of authentic prison stuff."

OFFICIAL PRISON RECORD

Received San Quentin 4/3/48 as #A-8811, Odlum, Jerome, from Los Angeles County for the crime of non-sufficient fund check and pr/fel for sentence of 0-14 years. Term fixed at 5 years. Parole when served two calendar years. Paroled 4/3/50. Discharged 4/3/53.

Peek. *This Is San Quentin: A Folio of Sketches Depicting the Complete History of the Nation's Largest Prison.* San Quentin, CA: San Quentin Prison, 1941, 40 p., illus, 1941.

Contents: Foreword; Early Days of the Convict Ship; The First Cell Block; Oddities from the Files; The State Takes Over; Black Bart; Early California Bandits; Counterfeiters of the Golden West; Indian Trade; Bad Women of the Barbary Coast; Hatchet Men of the Eighties; Cruelty on the High Seas; Arson Wave as the Century Turned; The Expansion Years—Modern Penal Administration; First Day of a "Fish"; Cell Life; Sunday Yard Scene; Oldtimers; Education Department; Vocational Training School; Hobby Shop; Submarine Nets; Cargo Nets; Transport Bunks; Getting Ready for Christmas; "Bum Beef"; *The News* (*San Quentin News*); Interview Time; Ship Fenders; Assault Boats; "Doing the Book"; Salvage Project; The Laundry; Alcoholics Anonymous; On the Air; The Gym; The 4th of July Fights; Blood Donors; The Canteen; Parole Procedure; Interstate Parole; The Prison That Grew From a Floating Dungeon to an Institution of Brilliant Social Rehabilitation.

Stanley, Leo Leonidas (M.D.), and Evelyn Wells. *Men at Their Worst.* New York: D. Appleton-Century, 1940, 322 p., illus.

The Scientific Book Club review claimed this book to be "A most engrossing story. Dr. Stanley's practical experience should guarantee him an audience not among sensation seekers, but among thoughtful people who are really concerned with the prison problem. He takes a middle course between the extremists that gives an air of common sense to his many deductions. Once cannot escape the fact that the many anecdotes and case histories that fill the pages are astonishing, but they point to sober medical and sociological conclusions."

Tasker, Robert Joyce. *Grimhaven.* New York: Alfred A. Knopf, 1928, 214 p., $3.

The author started to serve an indeterminate sentence for robbery at San Quentin at the age of 21. Mr. W. D. Lane, who reviewed this book, said, "It is a life-like and vivid picture of prison life. To me the book is genuine—I sense the honesty of its feeling and the straightforwardness of its purpose. Tasker has lived through the things that do not count; he has set down the things that were of permanent importance to him." Another reviewer claimed that "Its own individual merits entitle it to mature consideration. It is the relentless baring of a soul, the pitiless analysis of life behind walls that are built to hide and do not shelter."

OFFICIAL PRISON RECORD

Received San Quentin 10/16/24 as #39962, Tasker, Robert J., from Alameda County for the crime of robbery first degree for an indeterminate sentence of 5 years to life. Term fixed at 10 years 12/7/29. Release on parole 12/10/29. Discharged 4/16/31. Granted pardon by Governor Culbert L. Olson 7/27/39.

Wilkins, James H. *Evolution of a State Prison...* Copy prepared by CLinton T. Duffy. Printed in *The Bulletin*, a San Francisco newspaper, extending from June 13, 1918 through July 10, 1918. San Quentin, CA: California State Prison, San Quentin, 1919, 96 mimeo bds.

Historical narrative of the 10 years from 1851-61, during the period when the care and employment of convicts was turned over to lessees, San Quentin's natal day and the first six months of its existence as a penitentiary for the incarceration of criminals, how legislative quarrels delayed the construction of modern prison buildings and horrors of the old prison ship were multiplied, dark days for prison lessee and an incident that illustrates triumph of wrong over right, peace officers in the pioneer days made handsome profits in transporting criminals to the penitentiary and in other ways when the opportunity offered, in 1854 the escape of convicts became so frequent that the people in the neighboring counties were terroized by depredations and threatening conduct, stories of irregularities at the prison caused the governor to order an investigation, the stories of female prisoners read like Boccaccio, legislative investigation showed that prison finances were in a deplorable condition while the guards and prisoners were given to excessive drinking at the bar, state drives hard bargain with Estell when he is compelled to relinquish control of San Quentin because of the insufficient facilities to house convicts, legislature creates a Board of Prison Directors to take possession of San Quentin without providing for paying the lessees' sum agreed upon as a compromise on claim, while the finances of the state were at a low ebb prisoners were not properly clothed or fed, a new Board of Directors appealed to legislature for help, the state's first experiment in managing the prison a costly affair especially the building of the wall which was scored by a legislative investigating committee, state management of San Quentin proved so disastrous that the legislature (on the report of a committee) again authorized a lease be given Estell, General Estell again gets into financial difficulties under his new lease because the state failed to live up to its agreement to pay him $10,000 a month, administration of the state's affairs from 1850 to 1861 was so crooked that the machinations of labor bosses shine like the efforts of disinterested and patriotic citizens, General Estell after many reverses sublets prison to a new contractor who makes money out of the exploitation of convict labor but who neglects the prisoners, state again takes control of the prison after the lessee has been forcibly ousted by order of the legislature, the courts try to protect the rights of

McCauley the lessee, McCauley's triumphant entry to San Quentin after the courts decided his dispossesion was not legal and the statute was unconstitutional, the legislature in its effort to oust the lessee of the prison gets into a further tangle from which they try to free themselves by offering the olive branch, McCauley and Tevis the lessees refuse a compromise for $200,000 but agree to take a larger sum which the solons finally agree to pay them, during McCauley's second administration he rules San Quentin like a feudal lord defies the power of the state to take any part in its affairs and makes his own laws, administration of prison affairs under the Lt. Governor results in revolts and breaks and finally in the establishment of a barbarous discipline, prejudice of the people and press against prisoners and ex-convicts is only gradually overcome by action of the parole law, the old order that virtually condemned a convict to a life of crime has gone for good under the able and humane policy of the present warden who has accomplished much good.

Turner, Ethel. *One-Way Ticket*. Harrison Smith, 1934, 321 p.

"A story of the great gray California prison, San Quentin. The father of Veronica Bourn is captain of the prison guards, with a house inside the reservation. The book tells of this little community of prison officials and their wives and families—a community whose days and nights are lived in the shadow of the prison, conditioned by what is going on there. Always in the background is the dread of what may happen should one of the desperate men confined within these grim walls escape...Ethel Turner is herself the daughter of a prison official and lived at San Quentin for 19 years."—*The New York Times*.

"Miss Turner's accurate observation of detail and her skill in describing the complicated relationships between prisoner and guard, guard and outsider, make up for an otherwise somewhat commonplace machinery of plot... While *One-Way Ticket* is more remarkable as a picture of the prison community at work than as a novel, largely because of this weakness, the best thing about it is the author's freedom from prejudice and social pleading either for or against the convicts."—*Saturday Review of Literature*.

INDEX

NOTE: All place names refer to California unless otherwise noted.

www.ingramcontent.com/pod-product-compliance
Lightning Source LLC
Chambersburg PA
CBHW031152270326
41931CB00006B/242
* 9 7 8 0 8 9 3 7 0 4 3 6 0 *